AA

D0270894

50 WALKS IN
The Cotswolds

50 WALKS OF 2–10 MILES

Contents

Contents

Rating

Each walk is rated for its relative difficulty compared to the other walks in this book. Walks marked ✚✚✚ are likely to be shorter and easier with little total ascent. The hardest walks are marked ✚✚✚

Walking in Safety

For advice and safety tips see page 176.

Locator Map

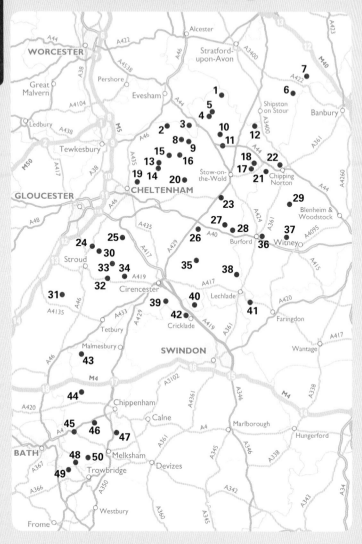

Legend

‒‒▶‒‒	Walk Route	▨	Built-up Area
❶	Route Waypoint	▨	Woodland Area
‒ ‒ ‒	Adjoining Path	🚻	Toilet
⧵⫽⧸	Viewpoint	P	Car Park
•	Place of Interest	🝔	Picnic Area
⌂	Steep Section	)(	Bridge

Introducing The Cotswolds

For many people the Cotswolds epitomise a vision of rural England. Here are pretty golden-stone villages, huddled in tranquil wooded valleys, bisected by sparkling brooks and surrounded by evergreen farmland. But for many too, this vision is unrealised. The crowds that throng around Broadway and Bourton-on-the-Water, buying their ice creams and enjoying the various tourist 'attractions' are surely missing something. Take a bit more time to explore this region and you will see that sometimes the myth and the reality can be reconciled, especially if you are prepared to step out of your car and get your boots muddy.

Protected

The whole region is protected by the Cotswolds Area of Outstanding Natural Beauty (AONB), at 790 square miles (2038sq km) the largest area in the country to be designated in this way. In the east, these 'official' Cotswolds reach surprisingly deep into Oxfordshire, to the north they point green fingers into both Warwickshire and Worcestershire, in the south, Wiltshire and North East Somerset claim their portions, but the lion's share of this beautiful landscape falls in Gloucestershire, and you will find this is where the majority of the walks in this guide are too.

Changing Scenery

Approaching the Cotswolds from the north-east, you'll notice the scenery begins to change in subtle ways. The half-timber and thatch of 'Shakespeare Country' begins to give way to a honey-coloured stone which defines the borders of the region. This is the oolitic limestone that tilts down from west to east. In the east the gradually rising profile is virtually indistinguishable. One is only vaguely aware that the surrounding countryside is gaining in altitude. This is open, arable farming country, punctuated by dark stands of trees and rivers flanked by water-meadows. Here you will find the source of the mighty Thames. Although the watershed is hardly apparent, the presence of two great east–west canals hints that it may have once presented a formidable obstacle to transport. These waterways – the Thames and Severn and the Kennet and Avon canals – provide some of the best level walking in the southern Cotswolds and cut through the very heart of the suddenly dramatic valleys that emerge on the western side.

PUBLIC TRANSPORT

There are good rail links to many of the towns which surround the Cotswolds and the Cotswold Line from London to Worcester and Hereford cuts through the northern part with several stops connecting to dedicated bus links. In the south, the railway line down the Avon Valley has some very convenient halts for walkers on the Kennet and Avon Canal. You can get train times from the national rail enquiry line on 08457 48 49 50. Outside these favoured places, travel by public transport can be a hit and miss affair with no through ticketing and some very poor connections. There is a bewildering array of operators and getting home again after a walk which finishes later than six o'clock in the evening can be difficult. For timetable information you should call the various county travel information lines. In Oxfordshire call 01865 810405, in Gloucestershire call 01452 425543 (24 hours), in Wiltshire call 08457 090899, in Warwickshire call 01926 414140. For other areas call Traveline on 0871 200 2233 (24 hours). You can also find details on the internet at www.pti.org.uk

Idyllic

But it is the idyllic stone-built villages that attract visitors to all parts of the Cotswolds, and on these walks you will find out why. In Snowshill, Bibury, Castle Combe and Stanton, the impossibly lovely buildings will take your breath away. And in Chipping Campden, you'll feel you have found the epicentre of this vernacular wealth. The townscapes are sublime too, as you'll find at Bradford-on-Avon, Corsham and Burford. There is an intimacy about these warm buildings which never fails to thrill and inspire locals and visitors alike. You will not be the first to experience the uplifting charm of the Cotswolds. Thousands of years ago ancient peoples were moved to commemorate the burial of their dead on these undulating hills. At Belas Knap, you'll find one of the best preserved remnants of such burials, and at the Rollright Stones you may wonder at what insights these early folk possessed when they lined up their megalithic arrays with the midsummer moon.

Fine Buildings

Vernacular architecture in the Cotswolds undoubtedly provides many of the stars of the built environment, but there are some grand houses too. There's nothing here on the scale of Longleat or Blenheim, but you'll find Sezincote and Compton Wynyates delightful nevertheless. Church buildings are also an impressive part

Using this book

INFORMATION PANELS

An information panel for each walk shows its relative difficulty (see Walk 5), the distance and total amount of ascent. An indication of the gradients you will encounter is shown by the rating ▲▲▲ (no steep slopes) to ▲▲▲ (several very steep slopes).

MAPS

Each walk in this book has a map and we also suggest which Ordnance Survey map you should take with you. The minimum time suggested is for reasonably fit walkers and doesn't allow for stops.

START POINTS

The start of each walk is given as a six-figure grid reference prefixed by two letters indicating which 100-km square of the National Grid it refers to. You'll find more information on grid references on most Ordnance Survey maps.

DOGS

We have tried to give dog owners useful advice about how dog friendly each walk is. Please respect other countryside users. Keep your dog under control, especially around livestock, and obey local bylaws and other dog control notices.

CAR PARKING

Many of the car parks suggested are public, but occasionally you may find you have to park on the roadside or in a lay-by. Please be considerate when you leave your car, ensuring that access roads or gates are not blocked and that other vehicles can pass safely.

of this legacy. The romantic remains of Hailes Abbey sit quietly at the foot of the escarpment and are best seen from the footpath near Beckbury Camp, where Thomas Cromwell surveyed their destruction for Henry VIII. Among the outstanding churches, Chipping Camden is a tribute to the wealth of the medieval wool trade and the twin churches at Eastleach Turville and Eastleach Martin eye each other across the River Leach.

Hill Country

Buildings and villages are not for everyone though and, at its western edge, the Cotswold escarpment can hold its own for lovers of wide views. From Dover's Hill down to Uley Bury, you'll see faraway Wales, the Forest of Dean and the Malvern Hills, as well as catching some fine panoramas of the Cotswolds themselves rising up from the Severn Plain and Vale of Evesham. The Cotswold Way National Trail follows this edge for much of its 101-mile (163km) route.

Historic Landscape

This is the land where Laurie Lee grew up, made famous by his evocative childhood memories in *Cider with Rosie*. Here Arts and Crafts pioneers rediscovered pre-industrial values in design and created everything from glassware to revolutionary gardens. A century before, the Industrial Revolution transformed the local woollen industry, bringing great mills to the Stroud Valley and poverty to the old weaving villages. Much of the Cotswolds' history is tied to the fortunes of wool. At one time this was the wool capital of Europe. The elaborate medieval churches are testimonies to the wealth of their merchant patrons. But you'll find precious few sheep on the hills now. Agricultural changes over the last century almost brought the local 'Cotswold Lion' breed to extinction. Now your only glimpse of these fine beasts might be in one of the rare breeds centres. While the stone walls and tight fields of pastoral farming survive on the poorer soils, arable dominates the Cotswold landscape.

Off the Beaten Path

Walk through this ever-changing landscape and see how little has actually changed over the centuries. The woods, the villages, the hidden valleys and surprising elevations remain. This apparent contradiction reflects the region's historical ability to reinvent itself and is why new generations of visitors will always discover the region for themselves. This selection of 50 walks introduces the themes and characters that created this living, beautiful landscape. It won't take you long to appreciate that the only way to enjoy the Cotswolds to the full is to step off the beaten path.

Overleaf: Arlington Row, Bibury (Walk 35)

Gardens Around Mickleton

A walk that takes you past Kiftsgate Court and Hidcote Manor Garden, two early 20th-century creations of international repute.

> **DISTANCE** 5 miles (8km)   **MINIMUM TIME** 2hrs 15min
>
> **ASCENT/GRADIENT** 625ft (190m) ▲▲▲   **LEVEL OF DIFFICULTY** +++
>
> **PATHS** Fields, firm tracks, some possibly muddy woodland, 5 stiles
>
> **LANDSCAPE** Woodland, open hills and villages
>
> **SUGGESTED MAP** OS Explorer 205 Stratford-upon-Avon & Evesham
>
> **START / FINISH** Grid reference: SP 162434
>
> **DOG FRIENDLINESS** On lead in livestock fields, good open stretches elsewhere
>
> **PARKING** Free car park at church
>
> **PUBLIC TOILETS** None en route

This walk takes you within striking distance of two of the finest planned gardens in the country. The first, Kiftsgate Court, is the lesser known of the two but nonetheless demands a visit. The house itself is primarily Victorian, while the garden was created immediately after World War One by Heather Muir, who was a close friend of Major Johnston, the creator of the nearby Hidcote Manor Garden. Kiftsgate's gardens are designed around a steep hillside overlooking Mickleton and the Vale of Evesham, with terraces, paths, flowerbeds and shrubs. The layout is in the form of rooms and the emphasis is more on the plants themselves, rather than on the overall design. The steeper part of the garden is almost a cliff. It's clad in pine trees and boasts wonderful views across the vale below.

Major Johnson's Rooms

The second horticultural treat is Hidcote Manor Garden, part of the little hamlet of Hidcote Bartrim. This garden is the fruit of more than 40 years of work by Major Lawrence Johnson, an East Coast American who purchased the 17th-century manor house in 1907 and gave it to the National Trust in 1948. Many people consider it be one of the greatest of English gardens, and certainly it is one of the most influential. Hidcote grew from almost nothing – when Major Johnson first arrived there was a just a cedar tree and a handful of beeches on 11 acres (4.5ha) of open wold. To some extent it reconciles the formal and informal schools of garden design. Hidcote is not one garden but several. Like Kiftsgate it is laid out in a series of 'outdoor rooms', with walls of stone and of hornbeam, yew and box hedge. These rooms are themed, having names such as the White Garden and the Fuchsia Garden. There is also a wild garden growing around a stream, as well as lawns and carefully placed garden ornaments that help to create a bridge between the order within and the disorder without.

Have a Butchers

This walk begins in Mickleton, at the foot of the Cotswold escarpment, below these two fine gardens. Clearly a Cotswold village, notwithstanding

MICKLETON

its mixture of stone, thatch and timber, the parish church at the village edge, lurks behind a striking house in the so-called Cotswold Queen Anne style. It has a 14th-century tower and a monument to the 18th-century quarry owner from Chipping Campden, Thomas Woodward. Near the hotel in the village centre is a Victorian memorial fountain designed by William Burges, the architect behind Cardiff Castle. There is also a fine butcher's shop here, a sight to behold, especially in autumn, when it's festooned with locally shot pheasant. This was also the birthplace of Endymion Porter, a patron of the Cotswold Olimpick Games on Dover's Hill (See Walk 4).

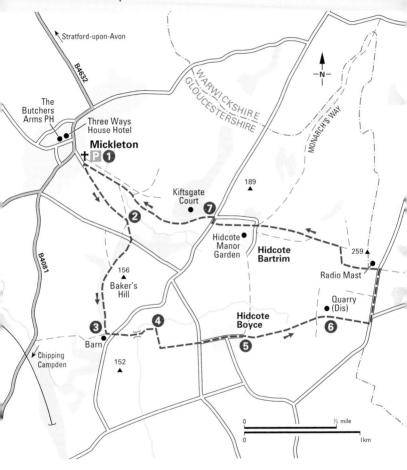

WALK 1 DIRECTIONS

❶ With your back to the church, turn right up a bank to reach a kissing gate to the left of Field House. Continue across a field on a right diagonal to a kissing gate at a thicket. Follow a path through trees and go through another kissing gate to emerge into a field and follow its left margin to reach a kissing gate at the end.

❷ In the next field go half right to a gate in the corner. Cross a road and go up some steps to a stile or a gate. Turn right to walk around the edge of the field as it bears left. After 250yds (229m), take a path among trees, a steep

13

WHILE YOU'RE THERE

It would be a shame to miss the two fine gardens. Kiftsgate Court is open May to July, Saturday to Wednesday 2–6, and April, and August to September on Sunday, Monday and Wednesday 2–6. Home-made teas are available but dogs are not welcome. Up the road, Hidcote Manor Garden is owned by the National Trust and is open daily, 10.30–6.30. It is closed Thursday and Friday, March to November, except June and July, when it's closed Friday only. There is a good restaurant and plant sales centre.

bank eventually appearing down to the right. The path brings you to a field and then a Dutch barn.

3 At the barn turn left briefly on to a track. Just about opposite the barn, keep left of a hedge, following the edge of a field to the bottom corner. Go through a gap to a bridge, with a stile on each side, across a stream and turn left.

WHAT TO LOOK OUT FOR

In Hidcote Boyce some of the houses, though built of stone broadly in the Cotswold style, are unusually tall. The style is almost unique to the village.

4 Follow the margin of the field as it goes right and then right again. Continue until you come to a field gate on the left. Go through this and walk until you reach another field gate at a road. Walk ahead through Hidcote Boyce. Where the road goes right, stay ahead to pass through a farmyard.

5 Beyond a kissing gate take a rising track for just over 0.25 mile (400m). Where this track appears to fork, stay to the left to enter a field via a field gate. Bear left and then right around a hedge and head for a field gate. In an area of grassy mounds stay to the left of a barn and head for a gate visible in the top left corner.

6 Follow the next field-edge to a road. Turn sharp left to follow the lesser road. Immediately before a radio transmission mast turn left on to a track and follow this all the way down to pass through Hidcote Manor Garden's car park entrance. Go straight on for 30 paces to turn left through a gate and then immediately right to walk a path parallel to the road with Hidcote's trees on your left. Through a beech copse enter a field through a kissing gate and cross it to a gate on the far side.

7 At the road turn right and then, before Kiftsgate Court, turn left through a gate and descend through a field. Pass through some trees and follow the left-hand side of the next field until you come to a gate on the left. Go through this and cross to another gate ignoring a footbridge to your left. Follow the edge of the next field to a gate. Go through this and head towards Mickleton church and a path between walled graveyards to return to the start via a gate.

WHERE TO EAT AND DRINK

In Mickleton the Butchers Arms serves good pub food, and the Three Ways House Hotel is recommended for its puddings in particular. It's the home of the famous 'Pudding Club', where you can taste the finest in traditional English desserts. There is also a restaurant at Hidcote Manor Garden and a tea room at Kiftsgate Court.

Left: The Water Garden, Kiftsgate Gardens (Walk 1)

Around Dumbleton Hill

Several centuries of church-building can be seen around Dumbleton Hill.

DISTANCE 8.75 miles (14.1km)	**MINIMUM TIME** 3hrs 45min

ASCENT/GRADIENT 427ft (130m) ▲▲▲ **LEVEL OF DIFFICULTY** +++

PATHS Mostly good paths, field tracks and village roads, 3 stiles

LANDSCAPE Gentle farmland and quiet villages

SUGGESTED MAP OS Explorer OL45 The Cotswolds

START / FINISH Grid reference: SP 039364

DOG FRIENDLINESS Mixed farming area, so off lead with discretion

PARKING On street near church in Wormington

PUBLIC TOILETS None en route

Wormington sits quietly away from the B4078, perhaps less busy now than in its first recorded mention in 1297. Today a hexagonal bench, ringing a splendid specimen tree, invites you to sit while donning your walking boots. Tucked behind this tiny green stands St Katharine's Church, a small, almost petite, building of 14th-century origin. It boasts a 9th-century stone crucifix, dug up in nearby Wormington Grange and said to have been salvaged from Winchcombe Abbey, and a stunning, 400-year-old brass depicting a mother and child in the lady's bed chamber.

Family Funded

Whereas St Katharine's is spire-less, having just a short bell-turret, the 200ft (61m) Victorian Gothic spire of St Andrew's Church in Toddington is visible from afar. On an ancient site among yew trees, the honey-stone building is largely the work of masons in the 17th, 18th and 19th centuries, funded by the Tracy family. The Tracy family also built the 17th-century Toddington House, all but demolished in living memory. The 2nd Baron Sudeley gave his name to the side chapel; this is his last resting place, with his wife, in a marble tomb. An inscription shows that the 6th Baron Sudeley was killed in action in 1941.

Gatehouse Remains

What remains of Toddington House is part of the gatehouse, and little more than a façade. You can see the remnants over the churchyard wall, to the left. Walk a little further round for sight of the magnificent Toddington Manor. This 19th-century Gothic mansion is undergoing extensive restoration.

Dumbleton's history goes back to Saxon times, although the oldest features apparent today are at St Peter's Church, primarily its arched north doorway. The church has undergone several additions and changes; some have suggested that the purpose of the 15th-century south aisle was to provide a place for Masses for the victims of the Black Death. Also of note in the church is the piscina (stone basin), over 600 years old. A hall was first built in Dumbleton in the 16th century. However, that was demolished

Right: Broadway Tower (Walk 3)

and the present-day Dumbleton Hall is the 1830 creation of G S Repton. He was commissioned by Edward Holland, the owner of the estate and founder of the Royal Agricultural College in Cirencester. Dumbleton Hall has a landscaped lake and, from the footpath, a variety of trees worthy of a small arboretum. The hall is now a 34-bedroomed hotel.

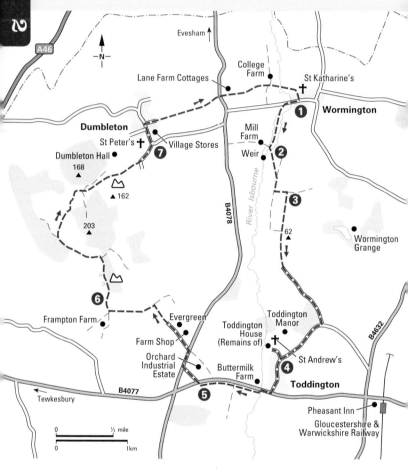

WALK 2 DIRECTIONS

❶ Walk west, on the road, to some power lines. Just after these take the footpath on the left. Pass through a gate, maintaining this line for a further 600yds (549m).

❷ Pass through a gate and turn left away from Mill Farm (view the waterwheel first), to cross the River Isbourne. Cross a narrow field, noting the mill's weir to your right and reach another gate.

Go diagonally across another field, under power lines again, turning right beside a fence that soon becomes hedgerow. In about 235yds (215m) turn left to walk along the right-hand field-edge. Within 160yds (146m) turn right.

❸ Follow this mud track – later a green lane and finally tarmac – for nearly 1 mile (1.6km), to a road junction. Turn right, passing the entrance of Toddington Manor, to reach a junction.

DUMBLETON HILL

WALK
2

4 Here a sign points to Toddington's church. Visit the church and view the ruin of Toddington House. Retrace your steps, then walk through Toddington village. At the main road turn right. Just after the pavement gives out (before Buttermilk Farm), cross over to a fingerpost and stile. Walk behind a screen of trees for 830yds (760m).

5 Re-cross the road to take the minor road through Orchard Industrial Estate. At the T-junction turn right. Go left, before the farm shop, up the driveway, passing the black-and-white effect farmhouse called 'Evergreen'. At the next T-junction turn left along a farm track, contouring the hill. As the track bends left to Frampton Farm bear right following a footpath sign.

6 Go ahead for about 30 paces, then turn hard right, uphill, on the Wychavon Way heading for a gate near trees. Once through this, the way soon steepens. On the brow join a stony track coming in from the right. On the way up there are good views back. Now on the level, continue for about 560yds (512m) to signposts at a junction of tracks. Follow 'Public Bridleway Dumbleton 1.25 miles', soon into a big, open field. A good track now leads all the way down to a minor road, then goes straight on past the driveway to Dumbleton Hall (a hotel).

7 Cross to the crucifix-style war memorial and turn left. Visit the church. About 41yds (37m) beyond Dairy Lane on the left, turn right along Blacksmiths Lane and then through a gate on the left to enter a field and skirt two field-edges. Cross the B4078 and, when the drive to Lane Farm Cottages bends left, go forward across one field to a gap in the hedge and then across another field to a stile. Cross the service road to College Farm and as it bends right, turn right across the field to cross over the small River Isbourne on a concrete bridge with corrugated iron sides. Pass under power lines and over a stile into pasture, then walk to the end of a breeze block barn wall. Turn right to a gate, rejoining the road in Wormington. The church is on the left.

William Morris's Broadway

*A haunt of the Arts and Crafts pioneer
towers above this Worcestershire village.*

WALK

3

DISTANCE *5 miles (8km)* **MINIMUM TIME** *2hrs 30min*

ASCENT/GRADIENT *755ft (230m)* ▲▲▲ **LEVEL OF DIFFICULTY** ✦✦✦

PATHS *Pasture, rough, tree-root path, pavements, 9 stiles*

LANDSCAPE *Flat vale rising to escarpment*

SUGGESTED MAP *OS Explorer OL45 The Cotswolds*

START / FINISH *Grid reference: SP 095374*

DOG FRIENDLINESS *Sheep-grazing country (some cattle and horses too)
so only off lead in empty fields; some stiles may be tricky*

PARKING *Pay-and-display, short stay, 4hrs maximum in Church Close,
Broadway; longer stay options well-signposted*

PUBLIC TOILETS *Church Close car park, country park and Fish Hill Picnic Place*

If Caspar Wistar were alive today, a springtime visit to Broadway would give him much pleasure. Visitors come in swarms to this Worcestershire village which lies against the edge of the Cotswolds – understandably, for it's one of the sweetest places in England. They buzz around a linear honeycomb, the honey-stone buildings stretching for the best part of a mile (1.6km). Horse chestnut trees flame with pinky-red candelabras and walls drip with the brilliant lilac flowers of wisteria. Caspar, the 18th-century American anatomist after whom the wisteria genus was named, would surely not miss this photo opportunity. (The fact that wisteria and pink horse chestnut are not 'authentic', as both were introduced to Britain centuries after Broadway's older buildings were constructed, doesn't seem to matter!) There are many buildings of note in Broadway, not least the partly 14th-century Lygon (pronounced 'Liggon') Arms. The Savoy Group bought it for £4.7 million in 1986. History has contributed to this price – in 1651 Oliver Cromwell stayed there on the night before the decisive clash in the Civil War, the Battle of Worcester.

Arts and Crafts

Less historic but more affordable is Broadway Tower. The 6th Earl of Coventry's four-storey folly (1799) has served as home to a printing press and a farmhouse, but is best known as a country retreat for William Morris (1834–96). Appropriately, in 1877 he founded the Society for the Protection of Ancient Buildings. Artistically, Morris empathised with the Pre-Raphaelite Brotherhood, a group, primarily of painters, founded in 1849 by William Holman Hunt. They believed that British art had taken a 'wrong turn' under the influence of Raphael, who, with Michelangelo and Leonardo da Vinci had made up the trio of most famous Renaissance artists. The English Pre-Raphaelites challenged the teachings of the establishment, producing vividly coloured paintings, lit unconventionally, which had an almost flat appearance.

BROADWAY

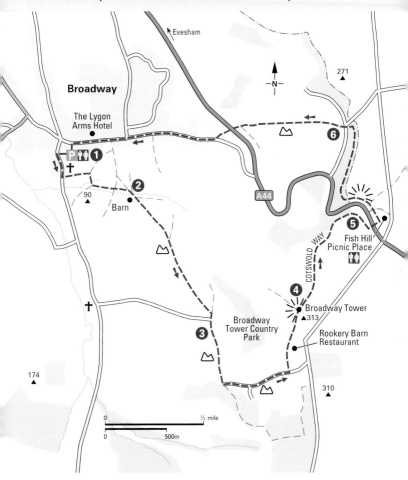

In 1859, Morris married Jane, an 18-year-old model for Dante Gabriel Rossetti, his British-born mentor. Rossetti's wife had committed suicide and Rossetti later had an affair with Jane. Morris and some friends (including Rossetti!) set up a company producing crafted textile and stained-glass products. Morris was fascinated by pre-industrial techniques. Disillusioned by the Industrial Revolution, he was attracted to Socialism in the 1870s. He joined the Social Democratic Federation and became increasingly militant writing extensively on Socialism and lecturing. All the while he was writing prose and poetry and, when Tennyson died in 1892, Morris was invited to succeed him as poet laureate. He declined and died four years later.

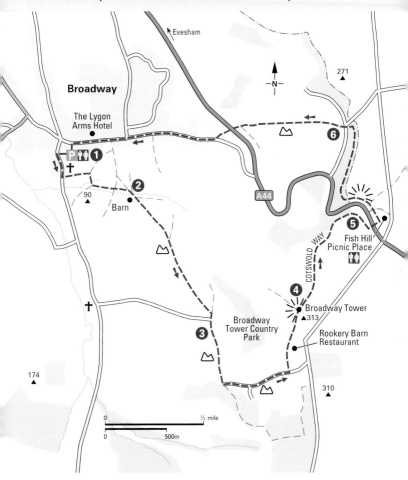

WALK 3 DIRECTIONS

❶ Walk back down Church Close then turn left. At the far end of the church wall turn left, soon passing a tiny, narrow orchard. Go through a gate before a strip of grass and turn immediately right to reach a simple stone bridge over a rivulet. Turn half left, across uneven pasture. Go to the right-hand field corner and pass through a kissing gate. In 35yds (32m) cross over a stile to reach a bridge of two railway sleepers beside a stone barn.

❷ Cross this to a waymarker through a boggy patch to two stiles. Maintain the line to another stile. Cross a large field to a stile, then continue in this direction following footpath signs across three more fields. In the third field go through the gate on the right side and cross a tree-lined track to a gate 62yds (57m) ahead.

❸ Slant uphill, passing in front of a stone bungalow. Just before the woodland ahead turn left. Join a tarmac road, steadily uphill. At the brow turn left over a stile, into Broadway Tower Country Park, and pass the Rookery Barn Restaurant. A tall kissing gate gives access to Broadway Tower.

WHILE YOU'RE THERE

The four flights of stairs up the Broadway Tower add interesting details about the already splendid view. Inside there are good displays about the history of the tower and the life of William Morris, and the group of craftsmen who settled in the Cotswolds and did much work in the area (fee; closed Monday to Friday from November to March).

❹ Beyond the tower go through a similar gate, then take the little gate immediately on the right. Move down, left, 22yds (20m) to walk in a hollow, through pasture and scrubby hawthorns, to a gate in a dry-stone wall. In 93yds (85m) meet a tractor track. Turn left and in 37yds (34m) go right by the Cotswold Way acorn marker. Walk parallel to the track in a similar hollow, aiming for some bright metal gates among trees. Beyond these go straight ahead and in 45yds (41m), at the next marker, bear right, walking above the road.

❺ Pass the first footpath sign leading to the road and follow the Cotswolds Way signs as the road bears right. Join a tarmac track parallel to the road past Broadway Quarry and soon meet the road. Cross it using the central refuge and reach Fish Hill Picnic Place. Continue to follow the Cotswold Way signs to the left, and up some steps to a trig point with good views. Follow the Limestone Trail signs ahead, entering a wood with a fence to the left. At the next signpost bear left down into a hollow and up the other side. At the top bear right, following a footpath sign, and leaving the Limestone Way. Follow this narrow path (beware many exposed tree roots) near the top of this dense wood. Eventually take steps on the left down to cross a road junction.

❻ Go over a stile to take the field path signposted 'Broadway'. Descend sweetly through pastures and over another stile. Swing left then right to pass over a stile, under the new road, emerging near the top end of the old one. Turn right, on to the dead end of Broadway's main street. In the centre, 60yds (55m) beyond two red telephone boxes, turn left, through Cotswold Court arcade, to Church Close car park.

WHERE TO EAT AND DRINK

Part-way round the route, the Rookery Barn Restaurant near Broadway Tower welcomes walkers. Apart from teas and coffees, call in here for simple meals. Dogs are welcome. You can sit outside, by the adjacent children's play area. Otherwise, options abound in busy Broadway.

Olimpick Playground Near Chipping Campden

Walk out from the Cotswolds' most beautiful wool town to Dover's Hill, the spectacular site of centuries-old Whitsuntide festivities.

DISTANCE 5 miles (8km))	**MINIMUM TIME** 2hrs
ASCENT/GRADIENT 280ft (85m) ▲▲▲	**LEVEL OF DIFFICULTY** ✚✚✚

PATHS Fields, roads and tracks, 8 stiles

LANDSCAPE Open hillside, woodland and village

SUGGESTED MAP OS Explorer OL45 The Cotswolds

START / FINISH Grid reference: SP 151391

DOG FRIENDLINESS Suitable in parts (particularly Dover's Hill) but livestock in some fields

PARKING Chipping Campden High Street or main square

PUBLIC TOILETS A short way down Sheep Street

The Cotswold Olimpicks bear only a passing resemblance to their more famous international counterpart. What they lack in grandeur and razzmatazz, however, they make up for in picturesqueness and local passion. Far from being one of the multi-million dollar shrines to technology which seem so vital to the modern Olympics, the stadium is a natural amphitheatre – the summit of Dover's Hill, on the edge of the Cotswold escarpment. The hill, with spectacular views westwards over the Vale of Evesham, is an English version of the site of the Greek original.

Royal Assent

Dover's Hill is named after the founder of the Cotswold Olimpicks, Robert Dover. Established with the permission of James I, they were dubbed 'royal' games, and indeed have taken place during the reign of 14 monarchs. Dover was born in Norfolk in 1582. He was educated at Cambridge and then was called to the bar. His profession brought him to the Cotswolds but he had memories of the plays and spectacles that he had seen in the capital.

The Main Event

It is accepted that the first games took place in 1612, but they may well have begun at an earlier date. It is also possible that Dover was simply reviving an existing ancient festivity. Initially, at least, the main events were horseracing and hare-coursing, the prizes being, respectively, a silver castle ornament and a silver-studded collar. Other competitions in these early games were for running, jumping, throwing, wrestling and staff fighting. The area was festooned with yellow flags and ribbons and there were dancing events as well as pavilions for chess and other cerebral contests.

Annual Event

The Olimpicks soon became an indispensable part of the local Whitsuntide festivities, with mention of them even being made in Shakespeare's work. Robert Dover managed the games for 30 years and he died in 1652. The

CHIPPING CAMPDEN

games continued in a variety of forms throughout the following centuries, surviving several attempts to suppress them when they became more rowdy and seemed to present a threat to public order and safety. They finally became an established annual event once again in 1966.

Nowadays, the games are a more like a cross between pantomime and carnival, but they have retained their atmosphere of local showmanship. At the end of the evening's events all the spectators, holding flaming torches, file down the road back into Chipping Campden, where the festivities continue with dancing and music along the main street and in the square.

The Wool Town

It's worth lingering in Chipping Campden, before or after the walk. Possibly the most beautiful of all the Cotswold towns, it was once famous throughout Europe as the centre of the English wool trade. A leisurely stroll along its curving High Street of handsome stone houses is a must. The church, too. is particularly fine and it's also worthwhile searching out the Ernest Wilson Memorial Garden, on the High Street.

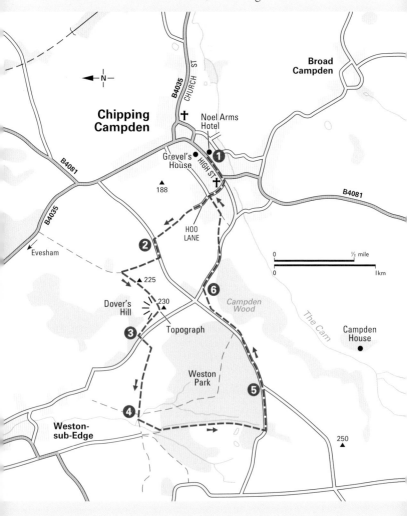

WALK 4 DIRECTIONS

❶ Turn left from the Noel Arms, continue to the Catholic church, and turn right into West End Terrace. Where this bears right, go straight ahead on Hoo Lane. Follow this up to a right turn, with farm buildings on your left. Continue uphill to a path and keep going to a road.

❷ Turn left for around 100 paces and then right to cross to a path. Follow this between hedges to a kissing gate. Through this turn left on to Dover's Hill, with extensive views before you, and walk along the escarpment edge, which drops away to your right. Pass a trig point and then a topograph. Now go right, down the slope, to a second kissing gate on the left.

WHILE YOU'RE THERE
Broadway Tower, with its associations with William Morris (See Walk 3), stands about 4 miles (6.4km) to the south west of Chipping Campden. A Gothic folly, built in Portland stone in 1799, there is an interesting small museum inside and fine views across the vale.

❸ Cross the road to a stile into a field. Cross this to a stile, then to a kissing gate by a horse shelter, then head to a gate in the bottom right-hand corner. Head straight down the next field. At a double stile go into another field and, keeping to the left of a fence, continue to another stile. Head down the next field, cross a track and then find adjacent stiles in the bottom left corner.

❹ Cross the first one and walk along the bottom of a field. Keep the stream and fence to your right and look for a double stile

and footbridge in the far corner. Go over, crossing the stream, and then turn left, following a rising woodland path alongside the stream. Enter a field through a gate and continue ahead to meet a track. Stay on this track, passing through gateposts and over a stile, until you come to a country lane and turn left.

WHERE TO EAT AND DRINK
Chipping Campden has plenty of pubs, tea rooms and restaurants. Badgers Hall, on the High Street, does an exceptionally fine tea, while the Eight Bells, on Church Street, is a very relaxing pub.

❺ After 400yds (366m) reach a busier road and turn left for a further 450yds (411m). Shortly before the road curves left, drop to the right on to a field path parallel with the road. About 200yds (183m) before the next corner go half right down the field to a road.

❻ Turn right, down the road. Shortly after a cottage on the right, go left into a field. Turn right over a stile and go half left to the corner. Pass through a kissing gate, cross a road among houses and continue into Birdcage Walk, then turn right to return to the centre of Chipping Campden.

WHAT TO LOOK OUT FOR
On reaching Dover's Hill, the route almost doubles back on itself in order to observe legal rights of way. Spend a little time poring over the topograph – on a clear day there is much to identify. In Campden, look out for the 14th-century Grevel's House, opposite Church Lane. William Grevel is thought to have been the inspiration for the merchant in *The Canterbury Tales*.

Arts and Crafts in the Campdens

A walk between Chipping and Broad Campden follows the rise and fall of the Guild of Handicraft.

DISTANCE 2.5 miles (4km)   **MINIMUM TIME** 1hr 15min

ASCENT/GRADIENT 83ft (25m) ▲▲▲   **LEVEL OF DIFFICULTY** ✦✦✦

PATHS Fields, road and track, 2 stiles

LANDSCAPE Farmland, hills, village

SUGGESTED MAP OS Explorer OL45 The Cotswolds

START / FINISH Grid reference: SP 151391

DOG FRIENDLINESS Suitable in parts but livestock in some fields

PARKING Campden High Street or parking area on main square

PUBLIC TOILETS Short way down Sheep Street

This walk starts in Chipping Campden, perhaps the finest of all Cotswold towns and extends to Chipping Campden's near neighbour, Broad Campden. Broad Campden does not have a spectacular high street, nor even much of a church, but it does have some exceptionally pretty houses (several of which, unusually for the Cotswolds, are thatched), an attractive pub and a 17th-century Quaker Meeting House, all in a snug, overlooked fold of the Cotswold countryside. It was here, in this idyllic rural setting, that Charles Ashbee set up his Guild of Handicraft.

Charles Ashbee

Born in Isleworth in Surrey, in 1863, Ashbee received his art education at King's College, Cambridge and was apprenticed to Bodley and Garner, a company specialising in Gothic revival architecture. As a consequence he became involved with, and subsequently a leader of, the burgeoning Arts and Crafts Movement, the leading light of which was the poet and artist William Morris. In 1888 Ashbee founded the Guild and School of Handicraft. Its educational programme laid great emphasis on training in the Arts and Crafts tradition with the prominence on furniture design.

Guild of Handicraft

Ashbee's work shows in its sparseness and restraint all the typical elements of the Arts and Crafts Movement. He also drew attention to the activities of other artists, notably he promoted the work of the Greene brothers and of Frank Lloyd Wright. In his essay *Should We Stop Teaching Art?* (1911) he discussed the changing nature of industrial patronage and organisation, reflecting his move towards reconciling the use of industrial methods.

The move to Chipping Campden in 1902 (and later to Broad Campden, where Ashbee converted a derelict Norman chapel into a place to live in 1905) was not an altogether successful one and by 1908 the Guild of Handicraft was no more – having fallen prey to competition from other cheaper producers like Liberty's. Ashbee died in 1942. However, the craft tradition he pioneered has not altogether died out. In Sheep Street

THE CAMPDENS

in Chipping Campden, where the original Guild shops stood just off the High Street, the silversmiths at David Hart's continue to produce beautiful, handcrafted work in the way that Ashbee would have approved of.

Alec Miller, a guildsman who came to Campden from Glasgow, describes the effect that his first sight of the town had on him; and somehow expresses the guiding principles of the Guild of Handicraft. 'I walked up Campden's one long street entranced and happy – a mile-long street with hardly a mean house, and with many of great beauty and richness... I could not 'read' the history embodied in these stone-built houses, so rich, so substantial and of such beautiful stone.'

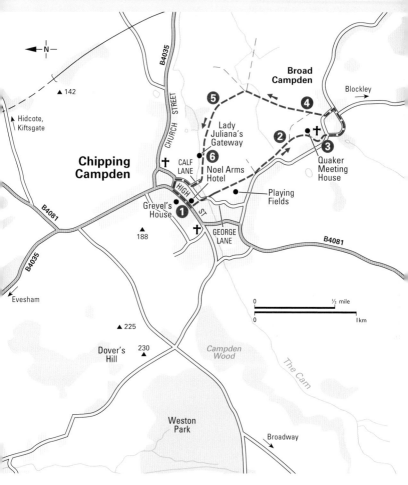

WALK 5 DIRECTIONS

❶ From Chipping Campden High Street, walk through the arch next to the Noel Arms Hotel and continue ahead to join a path. Pass some playing fields through a gate and at a junction with a road go left into a field and then quickly right to follow the edge of the field parallel with the road.

❷ After 600yds (549m), fork right and come to a kissing gate. Follow a drive, walk past a house and then cross the drive to a

WALK 5

gate. Pass through into an alley and follow it to pass the Quaker Meeting House.

❸ Emerge at the green with the church to your left. At a junction, continue ahead to walk through the village passing the Malt House. The road bears left and straightens. After the turning for Blockley, go left down a road marked 'Unsuitable for Motors'. After 70yds (64m) turn right along the drive of 'Hollybush'; a stone wall is to your left. After two stiles continue along the left, lower margin of an orchard.

❹ Go through a kissing gate, then cross a bridge and turn sharp right to walk along the right edge of a field, with the stream on the right. Go right to the end of the field to cross the stream and in the next field go straight across, bearing a little right, to a gap. Go up the centre of the next field to a kissing gate and cross into a field.

❺ Turn left and then go half right to pass to the right of a house. Through a kissing gate go half right to another. Go through and head quarter right down to another kissing gate in the corner. In the next field go half right, with a tree-lined stream on your right and Campden church away to the right, to a stream near a stone arch, Lady Juliana's Gateway.

❻ Do not cross the stream but, 70yds (64m) after the arch, turn right through a gate past a former watermill and follow the path as it turns left to a drive. Turn right and follow the drive to a road (Calf Lane). At the road turn right and at the top turn left into Church Street (turn right to visit the church) to return to a junction with the main street.

Perfect Mansion at Compton Wynyates

*Enjoy spectacular views of one of Warwickshire's
finest houses on this scenic walk over high ground.*

DISTANCE 6 miles (9.7km)   **MINIMUM TIME** 2hrs 30min

ASCENT/GRADIENT 298ft (90m) ▲▲▲   **LEVEL OF DIFFICULTY** +++

PATHS Field paths, tracks and roads, 9 stiles

LANDSCAPE Undulating countryside on edge of Cotswolds

SUGGESTED MAP OS Explorer 206 Edge Hill & Fenny Compton

START / FINISH Grid reference: SP 338437

DOG FRIENDLINESS On lead or under control across farmland

PARKING Spaces in Tysoe

PUBLIC TOILETS None en route

Regarded as one of the most visually striking mansions in England and described by Pevsner as 'the most perfect picture-book house of the Early Tudor decades', Compton Wynyates is all that remains of the village of Compton-in-the-Hole, which was depopulated by Sir William Compton during the reign of Henry VIII. The reason was simple. Sir William wanted to create a spacious park around his new home, built in brick on the site of an earlier structure, and the village was in the way.

Compton Wynyates

Lying in a secluded fold of the hills, about 12 miles (19km) south-east of Stratford-upon-Avon, Compton Wynyates first came into the possession of Philip de Compton in about 1204 and has been in the same family ever since. The original moated house was demolished and a new brick and stone building begun in about 1481 by Edmund de Compton, part of which still survives in the vicinity of the courtyard. The rebuilding of Compton Wynyates took about 40 years to complete.

The house passed to Edmund's son who, at the end of the 15th century, was a young page to Prince Henry. He was knighted by Henry VIII following the Battle of Tournai in 1512 and, as a gesture of thanks, the King also gifted him the old castle at Fulbroke, near Warwick. However, so keen was the Compton family to improve and enlarge Compton Wynyates that the castle was soon demolished to provide extra materials. Undoubtedly, the timber roof of the hall and the oriel window facing the courtyard came from Fulbroke. Many other distinguished features from that period include the battlemented towers and the great porch, which has the arms of Henry VIII and Catherine of Aragon above the door.

The variety of colour in the brickwork is breathtaking, with hardly two bricks being the same shade. As you look down the drive towards the house, you should catch a hint of pale rose, orange, dark red and blue. Henry VIII stayed here on several occasions, as did Elizabeth I, James I and Charles I, but it was during the Civil War that Compton Wynyates experienced its darkest days. The house was besieged and finally captured

COMPTON WYNYATES

by the Parliamentarians before eventually being returned to the Compton family. The church was completely demolished at the time and this period in Britain's history left deep scars on Compton Wynyates.

Secret Passages

Privately owned and sadly not open to the public, Compton Wynyates comprises a fascinating network of secret passages, hidden rooms and fine stairways. It is said there are almost 100 rooms and about 300 windows. The dining room has a fine Elizabethan, or perhaps early Jacobean, ceiling and there are many portraits in the house of Compton ancestors. Carved panels depicting the Battle of Tournai and a 16th-century tapestry of Cupid picking grapes are among many other historic features.

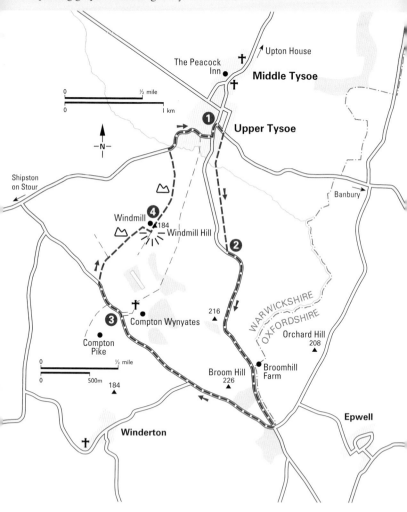

WALK 6 DIRECTIONS

① Make for the southern end of Upper Tysoe and look for the

turning signposted 'Shenington and Banbury'. Follow the road, keeping Middleton Close on the left, and turn right just before the speed derestriction signs at a gate and footpath sign. Keep alongside allotments, then the field boundary to a kissing gate in the corner and continue across the field to the next stile. Keep ahead in the next field, passing under power lines, and make for a plank bridge and stile in the boundary hedge. Go straight on up the field slope and, on reaching the brow of the hill, look for a stile and plank bridge in the hedge by the road.

❷ Turn left and follow the road as it curves right and up the hill. Pass Broomhill Farm and continue ahead to the first crossroads. Turn right here, signposted 'Compton Wynyates', and pass a turning on the left to Winderton. Follow the lane along to the main entrance to Compton Wynyates on the right.

❸ Keep walking ahead, passing a house on the left-hand side and, as the road begins to curve left, look for a galvanised gate and stile on the right. Join the green lane and follow it to the next gate and stile. Continue ahead and, when the track curves to the left, go straight ahead over a stile and up the edge of the field. Pass a ruined stone-built barn and make for the top corner of the field. Take some steps up the bank before climbing steeply but briefly up to a stile. Keep a stone wall and a restored

windmill on your left-hand side and look over to the right for a splendid view of Compton Wynyates house.

❹ Make for a stile a few paces ahead and then follow the path over the high ground, keeping to the right of the windmill. Make for a hedge corner ahead, pass through the gap and then descend the field slope, keeping the hedge on your right. Pass into the next field and keep close to the right-hand boundary. Aim a little to the left of the bottom right corner of the field and make for a stile leading out to the road. Turn right and return to the centre of Tysoe.

Edge Hill and a Theatre of War

Climb a spectacular wooded escarpment and enjoy fine views over a Civil War battleground.

DISTANCE 3.5 miles (5.7km)	**MINIMUM TIME** 1hr 30min
ASCENT/GRADIENT 280ft (85m) ▲▲▲	**LEVEL OF DIFFICULTY** +++

PATHS Field and woodland paths, country road, 2 stiles

LANDSCAPE Edge Hill escarpment

SUGGESTED MAP OS Explorer 206 Edge Hill & Fenny Compton

START / FINISH Grid reference: SP 370481

DOG FRIENDLINESS On lead in Radway and Ratley, under close control on Centenary Way

PARKING Radway village

PUBLIC TOILETS None en route

The scene may look peaceful now but just over 360 years ago the fields below the tree-lined escarpment known as Edge Hill were anything but quiet. This tranquil corner of south Warwickshire was the setting for the first major battle of the Civil War in 1642.

The Battle of Edge Hill

On the morning of Sunday 23 October Charles I's army departed from Cropredy Bridge, a few miles away in neighbouring Oxfordshire, arriving at Edge Hill, which was already occupied by Prince Rupert's army, at noon. A staggering 14,000 Royalist troops spread out across the entire hillside, from the Knowle to Sunrising Hill, and as many as 10,000 Parliamentarians, under the command of the Earl of Essex, were massed in the fields below. Led by Prince Rupert, the cavalry of the King's right flank charged and routed the enemy, pursuing the men beyond the village of Kineton, several miles to the north-west. They began to celebrate.

Driven Back

Elsewhere, the Royalists were not doing so well. Commanding the left flank, the Commissary-General attacked the enemy's right. At first, his efforts proved successful but on reaching a line of hedgerows and ditches near Little Kineton, he was driven back. At the same time the King advanced his centre, also with success, until he, too, was forced to halt – his way blocked by trees and hedges. The Royalist army suffered many casualties.

Open to attack on both sides, the centre gave way and the Royal standard-bearer, Sir Edmund Verney, was killed. The standard was subsequently taken, though later recovered. Prince Rupert re-emerged from Kineton and relieved the King's centre, thus avoiding defeat. The battle still raged as darkness descended over the escarpment and the Earl of Essex and his forces withdrew to Kineton for the night. The King slept in a nearby barn and then breakfasted in Radway the following morning. Neither side seemed keen to continue the battle and the King resumed his march to London unopposed while Essex withdrew to Warwick. Inconclusive though it was, the battle claimed the lives of over 4,000 men that day; 1,200 of them were buried by the vicar of Kineton.

There were occasions during the Civil War when it looked as if Charles might win. But two factors ruined his chances. One was the military genius of Oliver Cromwell, whose successes at Marston Moor (1644) and Naseby (1645) confirmed him as the foremost cavalry leader, and the other was the intervention of the Scots. The first Civil War finally ended in 1646.

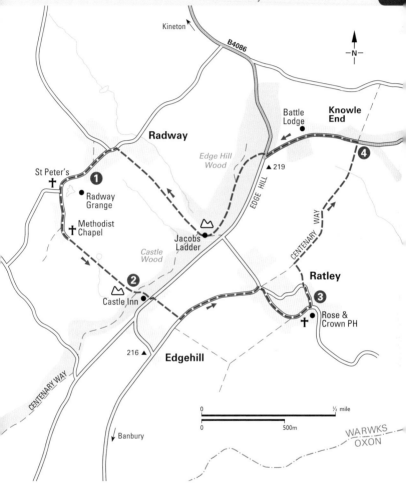

WALK 7 DIRECTIONS

❶ Walk through the village of Radway to the church. Veer left here into West End and pass alongside the grounds of Radway Grange on your left. Curve left by a pond and some thatched cottages. The 19th-century

Methodist chapel can be seen here. Follow the lane as it becomes a stony track and go through two kissing gates into a field. Walk ahead to a third gate and continue ahead across the sloping field towards Radway Tower, now the Castle Inn. Look for an inspection cover near the

left-hand field boundary and maintain the same direction, climbing steeply towards the wooded escarpment.

❷ Make for a gate and enter the wood. Continue straight over the junction and follow the markers for the Macmillan Way up the slope to the road. With the Castle Inn on your right, turn left for several paces to take a right-hand path running between Cavalier Cottage and Rupert House. Turn left at the road and walk along to Ratley. At the T-junction turn right and follow the High Street down and round to the left. Pass the church and keep left at the triangular junction.

❸ With the Rose & Crown over to your right, follow Chapel Lane and, when it bends left, go straight ahead up some steps to a stile. Keep the fence on the left initially before striking out across the field

to a stone stile in the boundary wall. Turn right and follow the Centenary Way across the field to a line of trees. Swing left and now skirt the field down to a galvanised kissing gate, cut across the field to a footbridge and then head up the slope to reach a gap in the field boundary.

❹ Turn left and follow the road past some bungalows. Pass Battle Lodge and make for the junction. Cross over and join a woodland path running along the top of the escarpment. On reaching some steps on the left, turn right and descend steeply via a staircase known as Jacobs Ladder. Drop down to a gate and then follow the path straight down the field to a kissing gate at the bottom. Go through a second kissing gate beyond it and then pass alongside a private garden to reach a drive. Follow it to the road and turn left for the centre of Radway.

Stanton, Laverton and Buckland

A walk through three radiant Cotswold villages,
two of which have strong connections with Methodism.

> DISTANCE 3.5 miles (5.7km)   MINIMUM TIME 1hr 30min
>
> ASCENT/GRADIENT 150ft (46m) ▲▲▲   LEVEL OF DIFFICULTY ✦✦✦
>
> PATHS Track, grassland, pavement, 9 stiles
>
> LANDSCAPE Grassland, wold, wide ranging views, villages
>
> SUGGESTED MAP OS Explorer OL45 The Cotswolds
>
> START / FINISH Grid reference: SP 067344
>
> DOG FRIENDLINESS Livestock in most parts of walk
>
> PARKING Car park in Stanton village at village hall (donation of £1)
>
> PUBLIC TOILETS None en route

Laverton is a large hamlet with many fine examples of Cotswold vernacular stone architecture. Buckland, though smaller, is a village with two particularly interesting buildings. The 15th-century rectory is the oldest medieval parsonage in Gloucestershire still in use. Although it can be admired only from the street, it has some fine stained glass and a timbered great hall. In the 18th century it was often used as a base by the founder of Methodism, John Wesley. Handsome Buckland Manor is now a hotel, while the neighbouring church contains medieval glass restored by William Morris, and a painted panel originally in Hailes Abbey, 5 miles (8km) to the south.

Stanton Court

Stanton was rescued from oblivion in 1906 by the architect Sir Philip Stott, who bought and restored Stanton Court, as well as many of the village's 16th-century houses. The church, on a lane leading from the market cross, has two pulpits – one dating from the 14th century, the other Jacobean – and a west gallery added by the Victorian restorer Sir Ninian Comper. John Wesley declaimed his message here in 1733. Stanton, in particular, is regularly used in period dramas for television and the cinema.

Spreading the Word

Methodism, the largest of the Protestant free Churches of Britain, originated among a group of devout 18th-century Oxford students under the influence of two brothers, John and Charles Wesley. As the name suggests, it is a radical and earnest creed, which arose out of dissatisfaction with the inadequacies of the established Church. The disillusionment of, in particular, John Wesley, was fostered by a missionary voyage to the American colonies in 1738. From then on he believed that he was destined to spread his beliefs – based on the idea of self-regeneration through faith, prayer and doing good works – across Britain.

He travelled about the country preaching in churches; and then, as bishops and churchmen became uneasy and banned him from the pulpit, he spoke at large, outdoor gatherings. His direct and 'methodical' approach clearly met with the approval of many a despairing congregation and in 1795 the movement, popular especially among the marginalised, lower ranks of society, was strong enough to secede from the Church of England. Needless to say, this was not enough for some and the Methodist movement fragmented into splinters of varying degrees of moderation or severity.

By 1932, however, most branches had rejoined the fold and the modern Methodist Church has about half a million members. In some ways the number of adherents does not reflect the level of shock and concern that the movement engendered among the Establishment of 18th-century Britain. And yet, even today, it is not unusual to find some still remote corner of countryside commemorated locally as a place where Wesley spoke.

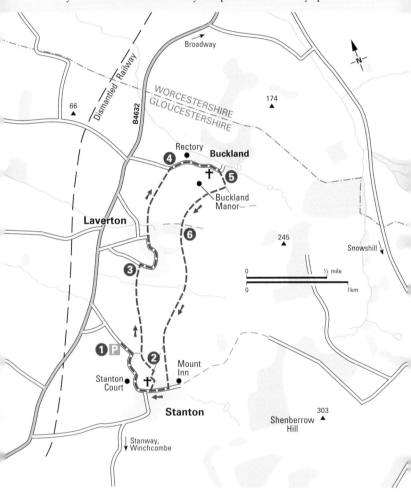

WALK 8 DIRECTIONS

❶ From the car park turn right and then left into the village by the war memorial plaque. Turn

left at Stanton village cross and head for the churchyard. Through a gate into the churchyard, pass to the right of the church and in the corner, turn right along an alley.

2 At the end turn left, just before a double gate, and follow a path to a kissing gate. Follow the left-hand margin of the field, heading towards a stile in a hedge gap. Cross the stile and turn quarter right to pass stables to your left. Go over another stile and at the next corner go through a gate, over a footbridge and through another gate to walk to a stile. Over this walk ahead and go over a stile just to the left of the field corner and continue, over another stile, towards Laverton.

WHAT TO LOOK OUT FOR
In Stanton, look for the dates and initials carved on the walls of some cottages, indicating the time of their construction and the name of the stonemason. Look too for Stanton Court, a Jacobean house that was owned and lived in by the saviour of the village, Sir Philip Scott.

3 Aim to the left of a house and, at the road, cross the stile and turn right. Follow the road through Laverton as it goes left, then left again and right. At a junction, beside a tree with a seat, cross over to enter a firm bridle path and follow this to the main street of Buckland.

4 Bear right and walk through the village, passing the rectory on your left-hand side (shortly after a telephone box and a public footpath sign) and then the church to the right. At the top, where the road curves left, go straight on to come to a kissing gate (to the right of a field gate).

5 Go through to a field and turn right. Pass Buckland Manor on the right and go through another two kissing gates.

WHERE TO EAT AND DRINK
There is one pub on the route – the Mount Inn in Stanton, which serves local beer and good food. Otherwise, the nearest centres are either Winchcombe or Broadway.

6 Continue along the contour path to go through a bridle gate and continue straight on. Pass through some trees to a kissing gate. Continue on the same line, passing through a gate, then over a footbridge between kissing gates. Continue, roughly along the contour, through a large field on the flank of the hill. Follow the prominent way markers and, after 0.25 mile (400m) cross a stile beside a gate and go straight ahead for another 0.25 mile (400m), partly through trees, to another stile. Cross this and go straight on, ignoring the path descending half right towards the church, until you come to a stile at the edge of Stanton. Go over this and bear right on to a drive which becomes a lane into Stanton village. Turn right through the village to return to the village hall car park.

WHILE YOU'RE THERE
Snowshill Manor, in the neighbouring village of Snowshill (See Walk 9) is filled with Japanese armour, musical instruments, farm implements, clocks and toys, and is definitely worth a visit. Stanway House, in the nearby village of Stanway, is the centre of a large estate owned by Lord Neidpath. The most striking feature of Stanway is the magnificent gatehouse to Stanway House, a gem of Cotswold architecture built c1630 by Timothy Strong of Barrington. Stanway House itself, is an outstanding example of a Jacobean manor house.

Stanton and Stanway from Snowshill

Discovering three of Gloucestershire's finest villages, which were saved from decline and decay.

DISTANCE 7 miles (11.3km)   **MINIMUM TIME** 2hrs 45min

ASCENT/GRADIENT 625ft (190m) ▲▲▲   **LEVEL OF DIFFICULTY** ✦✦✦

PATHS Tracks, estate grassland and pavement, 1 stile

LANDSCAPE High grassland, open wold, wide-ranging views and villages

SUGGESTED MAP OS Explorer OL45 The Cotswolds

START / FINISH Grid reference: SP 096341

DOG FRIENDLINESS On lead – livestock on most parts of walk

PARKING Snowshill village (free car park to north of the village)

PUBLIC TOILETS None en route

Villages in the Cotswolds are excellent examples of English vernacular architecture, but they have not always been prosperous. Many, like Stanton and Snowshill, were owned by great abbeys, but they passed to private landlords after the dissolution of the monasteries. Subsistence farmers were edged out by short leases and enclosure of fields. Villagers who had farmed their own strips of land became labourers. The number of small farmers decreased dramatically and, with the onset of the Industrial Revolution, so too did the demand for labour. Cheaper food flooded in from overseas and catastrophic harvests compounded the problem.

To the Cities

People left the countryside in droves to work in the industrial towns and cities. Cotswold villages, once at the core of the most important woollen industry in medieval Europe, gradually became impoverished backwaters. But the villages themselves resisted decay. Unlike villages in many other parts of Britain, their buildings were made of stone. Enlightened landlords, who cherished their innate beauty, turned them into restoration projects.

Enlightened Landlords

The three villages encountered on this walk are living reminders of this process. Snowshill, together with Stanton, was once owned by Winchcombe Abbey. In 1539 it became the property of Henry VIII's sixth wife, Catherine Parr. The manor house was transformed into the estate's administrative centre and remained in the Parr family until 1919. Then the estate was bought by Charles Wade, a sugar plantation owner. He restored the house and devoted his time to amassing an extraordinary collection of art and artefacts, which he subsequently bequeathed to the National Trust. Now forming the basis of a museum, his collection, from Japanese armour to farm machinery, is of enormous appeal. Next on this walk comes Stanway, a small hamlet at the centre of a large estate owned by Lord Neidpath. The most striking feature here is the magnificent gatehouse to the Jacobean Stanway House, a gem of Cotswold architecture built around 1630.

Restored Houses

The village of Stanton comes last on this walk. It was rescued from decay and oblivion in 1906 by the architect Sir Philip Stott. He bought and restored Stanton Court and many of the village's 16th-century houses. The peaceful parish church is located along a lane leading from the market cross. It has two pulpits (one dating from the 14th century, the other Jacobean) and a west gallery added by the Victorian restorer Sir Ninian Comper.

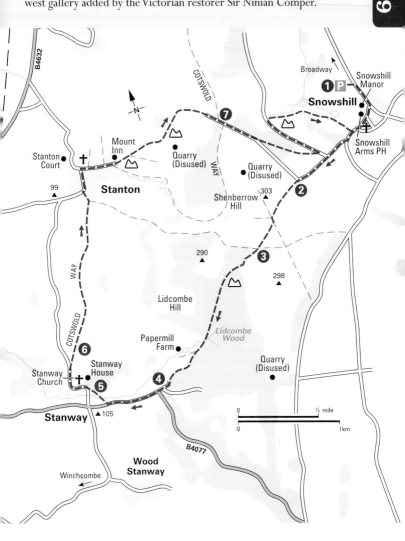

WALK 9 DIRECTIONS

❶ From the free car park walk into Snowshill village, descending to the right at a Y-junction past Snowshill Manor and the church on your left. After a 0.25-mile (400m) climb turn right down a lane signed 'Sheepscombe House'. After another 0.25 mile (400m) at a right-hand bend on the crest of the hill turn left up to a gate and enter a field.

❷ Go half right to a gate. In the next field go half right to the far corner and left along a track. Take the second footpath on the right through a gate into a field and walk half left to another gate. Cross straight ahead through the field to another gate on to a track.

❸ Ignore the footpath to your right, walk down a stony track with a wood on your right. After 275yds (251m) turn right on to a stony track, veering right just before a stone barn. The track descends steeply through Lidcombe Wood. After 0.5 mile (800m), where it flattens out, a farm comes into view across fields to the right, after which the track bears left uphill. Continue straight along the track, which becomes a narrow footpath, to a road.

❹ Walk along the pavement and, after 500yds (457m), turn right through a gate into a small orchard. Walk half left across this, bearing slightly right, to arrive at a kissing gate. Go through this and walk with a high wall to your right, to reach a road.

❺ Turn right and pass the impressive entrance to Stanway House and Stanway church, both on your right. Follow the road as it goes right. Shortly after another entrance turn right through a gate opposite a thatched cricket

pavilion. Go half left to another stile and in the next large field go half right.

❻ Now walk all the way into Stanton, following the regular and clear waymarkers of the Cotswold Way. After 1 mile (1.6km) you will arrive at a gate at the edge of Stanton. Turn left along a lane to a junction. Turn right here and walk through the village, turning right at the war memorial. Where the road goes left, walk straight on, passing the stone cross and then another footpath. Climb up to pass to the right of the Mount Inn. Beyond it walk up a steep, shaded path to a gate. Then walk straight up the hill on a stony track (ignoring a path to the right after a few paces). Climb all the way to the top to meet a lane, passing through two gates.

❼ Ignore the 'Cotswold Way' sign and walk down the lane for 250yds (229m) then turn left through a kissing gate into woodland. Follow the path, going left at a fork. At the bottom cross a stile, continuing in the field to a kissing gate in the far corner by the road. Pass through and turn left and walk for 600yds (549m). Before a cottage turn right through a gate into a scrubby field. Descend steeply to the far side and turn right through a gate. Continue to a stile on your right, cross it and turn left. Follow the margin of this grassy area to a track, then a gate and then follow the path back into Snowshill.

Blockley, Batsford and the Arboretum

*The exotic legacy of a 19th-century diplomat
adorns this part of the Cotswold escarpment.*

DISTANCE 5 miles (8km) **MINIMUM TIME** 2hrs 15min

ASCENT/GRADIENT 410ft (125m) ▲▲▲ **LEVEL OF DIFFICULTY** ✦✦✦

PATHS Lanes, tracks and fields, 7 stiles

LANDSCAPE Woodland, hills with good views and villages

SUGGESTED MAP OS Explorer OL45 The Cotswolds

START / FINISH Grid reference: SP 165348

DOG FRIENDLINESS Some good lengthy stretches without livestock

PARKING In village street to west of church, north of post office

PUBLIC TOILETS On edge of churchyard, just off main street in Blockley

---

England seems to be a country of trees. Walking through Gloucestershire you are surrounded by many native species but, when you visit Batsford Arboretum, you will encounter 50 acres (20.3ha) of woodland containing over 1,000 species of trees and shrubs from all over the world, particularly from China, Japan and North America. Public access to the arboretum is only possible via the A44 between Moreton-in-Marsh and Bourton-on-the-Hill, not from Batsford village itself.

The Japanese Connection

The arboretum was originally a garden created in the 1880s by the traveller and diplomat, Bertie Mitford, 1st Lord Redesdale and grandfather to the renowned Mitford sisters. Posted as an attaché to the British Embassy in Tokyo, he became deeply influenced by the Far East. Throughout the park there are bronze statues, brought from Japan by Bertie Mitford, and a wide range of bamboos. After the 1st Lord Dulverton purchased Batsford in 1920, his son transformed the garden into the arboretum we see today, with its 90 species of magnolia, maples, cherry trees and conifers. Batsford village is comparatively recent, having grown up at the gates of Batsford Park, a neo-Tudor house built between 1888 and 1892 by Ernest George. He built it for Lord Redesdale to replace an earlier, Georgian house. (It is not open to the public but is clearly visible from the arboretum.) Batsford church was constructed a little before the house, in 1862, in a neo-Norman style. It has several monuments to the Mitford family and a fine work by the sculptor Joseph Nollekens from 1808.

Silky Blockley

This walk starts in the unspoilt village of Blockley. It was originally owned by the bishops of Worcester but it didn't really begin to prosper until the 19th century. At one time no fewer than six silk mills, with over 500 employees, were driven by Blockley's fast-flowing stream. Their silks went mostly to Coventry for the production of ribbon. Blockley's history is both enlightened and superstitious. It was one of the first villages in the

41

BLOCKLEY

world to have electric light: in the 1880s Dovedale House was illuminated through Lord Edward Spencer-Churchill's use of water to run a dynamo. In the early part of that same century the millenarian prophetess, Joanna Southcott, lived in the village until her death in 1814. The tower of Blockley's substantial church predates the silk boom by only 100 years or so, but inside the church are several imposing monuments to the owners of the local mansion, Northwick Park. At least two of these are by the eminent 18th-century sculptor, John Michael Rysbrack (1694–1770).

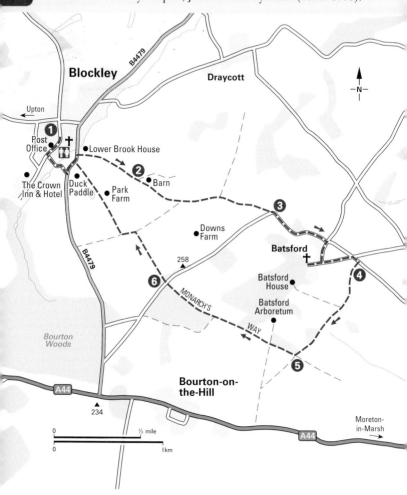

WALK 10 DIRECTIONS

1 Leave the churchyard by the tower and walk through the village, turning left at School Lane. Follow this down across a stream and up to the main road. Turn left and, just before Lower Brook House, turn right on to

a lane walking up for 0.25 mile (400m) until the lane bears left.

2 Continue ahead to pass to the right-hand side of a barn. In the next field follow its right-hand boundary to another gate. Pass through this to stay on the left side of the next field. Pass into yet

BLOCKLEY

another field and then after 0.3 miles (480m) go half right to a gate leading out to a road.

3 Go straight on and follow the road down to a crossroads. Turn right to pass through Batsford to a junction from where you can visit the church on the right. After visiting the church retrace your steps (there is no public access to the Arboretum from the village) to the junction and walk down the lime avenue then, at the next junction, turn right.

4 After 100 paces turn right on to a footpath and follow this through a succession of fields, negotiating stiles and gates where they arise. Batsford House will be visible above you to the right.

5 Finally, go through a gate into a ribbed field and turn right to a gate and kissing gate just left of a gate lodge at a drive. Cross this (the entrance to Batsford Arboretum), pass through a gate and follow the path up the field to a stile. Cross and continue to a track. Follow this up until where it bears left. Turn right on to a path and almost immediately left at a wall, to continue the ascent with the park wall on your right. Keep going until you reach a stile to a road.

6 Cross the road on to a track, then go through a gate and pass through two fields until you come to a path among trees. Turn left, go through another gate, and, after 140 paces, turn right over a stile into a field with Blockley below you. Continue down to a stile at the bottom. Cross into the next field and pass beneath Park Farm on your right. Go to the right of a pond to descend to a gate and stile, then follow a lane along the Duck Paddle, until you come to a road. Turn right and return to your starting point in the village.

The Nabob of Sezincote and Bourton-on-the-Hill

Discovering the influences of India through the Cotswold home of Sir Charles Cockerell.

DISTANCE 3 miles (4.8km)   **MINIMUM TIME** 1hr 30min
ASCENT/GRADIENT 85ft (25m) ▲▲▲   **LEVEL OF DIFFICULTY** ✚✚✚
PATHS Tracks, fields and lanes, 7 stiles
LANDSCAPE Hedges, field and spinney on lower part of escarpment
SUGGESTED MAP OS Explorer OL45 The Cotswolds
START / FINISH Grid reference: SP 175324
DOG FRIENDLINESS Under close control – likely to be a lot of livestock
PARKING Street below Bourton-on-the-Hill church, parallel with main road
PUBLIC TOILETS None en route

For anyone with a fixed idea of the English country house, Sezincote will come as a surprise. It is, as the poet John Betjeman said, 'a good joke, but a good house, too'. Built on the plan of a typical large country house of the era, in every other respect it is thoroughly unconventional. A large copper onion dome crowns the house, while at each corner of the roof are finials in the form of miniature minarets. The walls are of Cotswold stone, but the Regency windows and decoration, owe a lot to Eastern influence.

Hindu Architecture

Sezincote is a reflection of the fashions of the early 19th century. Just as engravings brought back from Athens had been the inspiration for 18th-century Classicism, so the colourful aqua-tints brought to England from India by returning artists, such as William and Thomas Daniell, were a profound influence on architects and designers. Sezincote was one of the first results of this fashion. Sir Charles Cockerell was a 'nabob', the Hindi-derived word for a European who had made their wealth in the East. On his retirement from the East India Company he had the house built by his brother, Samuel Pepys Cockerell, an architect. The eminent landscape gardener Humphry Repton helped Cockerell to choose the most picturesque elements of Hindu architecture from the Daniells' drawings.

Pavilion Inspiration

Some modern materials, like cast iron, were thought to complement the intricacies of traditional Mogul design. The garden buildings took on elements from Hindu temples, with a lotus-shaped temple pool, Hindu columns supporting a bridge and the widespread presence of snakes, sacred bulls and lotus buds. The Prince of Wales was an early visitor. The experience obviously made some impression as the intensely Mogul-influenced Brighton Pavilion arose not long after. Betjeman was a regular guest at Sezincote during his undergraduate days. 'Stately and strange it stood, the nabob's house, Indian without and coolest Greek within, looking from Gloucestershire to Oxfordshire.'

SEZINCOTE

Measuring Up in Bourton-on-the-Hill

This walks begins and ends in Bourton-on-the-Hill, a pretty village that would be exceptional were it not for traffic streaming through it on the A44. Nevertheless, there is quite a lot to see here. The church owes its impressive features to the fact that the village was formerly owned by Westminster Abbey, whose income was handsomely supplemented by sales of wool from their vast flocks on the surrounding hills. There is a fine 15th-century clerestory, lighting an interior notable for its substantial nave columns and a rare bell-metal Winchester Bushel and Peck (8 gallons/35.2 litres and 2 gallons/8.8 litres respectively). These particular standard English measures date from 1816, but their origins go back to the 10th century when King Edgar (reigned AD 959–975) decreed that standard weights be kept at Winchester and London. They were used to settle disputes, especially when they involved tithes. Winchester measures finally became redundant in 1824 when the Imperial system was introduced, though many Winchester equivalents remain in the United States. Further down the village, the 18th-century Bourton House has a 16th-century barn in its grounds.

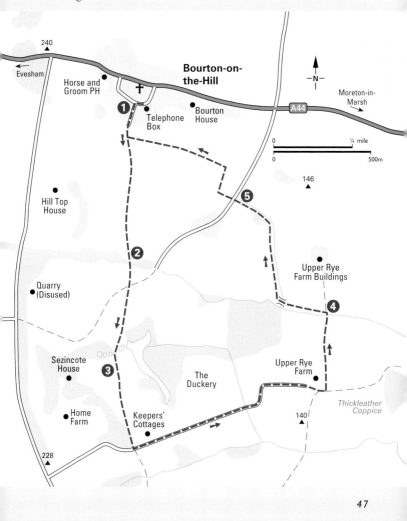

WALK 11 DIRECTIONS

1 Walk up the road from the telephone box with the church to your right. Turn left down a signposted track between walls. Go through a gate into a field and then continue forward to pass through two more field gates.

WHILE YOU'RE THERE

Both Sezincote and Bourton House are open to the public but have a limited season, so check their opening hours in advance. Batsford Arboretum and Falconry is only a mile (1.6km) away, just off the road to Moreton-in-Marsh.

2 Continue to a stile, followed by two kissing gates amid a tree belt. This is the Sezincote Estate – go straight ahead, following markers and crossing a drive. Dip down, keeping to the right of woodland, to two field gates among trees, with ponds on either side. Go ahead into a field, from where Sezincote House is visible to the right.

3 Walk into the next field via a gate and go right to the end, aiming for the top, right-hand

WHAT TO LOOK OUT FOR

As you start the walk look for a 'hole in the wall' just after the first gate. It consists of a tap located behind wooden doors just above ground, with the words 'Deo Gratias AD 1919', inscribed in the wall above. I presume this is in gratitude for the end of World War One. After Sezincote, as you walk down the road towards the farm, look for the buildings of the Fire Service Technical College, the main training centre for firefighters in the country.

corner. Pass through a field gate and kissing gate to a narrow road and turn left. Walk down this road, passing the keepers' cottages to your left, and through a series of three gates. The road will bottom out, curve left and right and bring you to Upper Rye Farm. Pass well to right of the farmhouse, go through a gate and, immediately before a barn, turn left along a track and a road.

4 After a second cattle grid, go left over a stile. Follow the left edge of the field to a footbridge between step-through stiles. Go over it and turn right. Now follow the right-hand margin of the field to a stile in the far corner. Cross this to follow a path through woodland until you come to step-through stiles on each side of a footbridge and a field and continue on the same line to another stile.

5 Cross a track to another stile into Sezincote's Millennium Oak Plantation and walk on. After a few paces, with Bourton-on-the-Hill plainly visible before you, turn right and follow the path to the next corner. Turn left and

WHERE TO EAT AND DRINK

The Horse and Groom is a handsome old pub at the top of the village. Recently refurbished, it serves good lunches. In Moreton-in-Marsh seek out the Marsh Goose, a restaurant specialising in good quality local produce.

pass through three gates. After the third one, walk on for 60 paces and turn right through a gate to return to the start.

The Lost Villages of the Ditchfords

A walk among the ghosts of former medieval agricultural communities, abandoned since the 15th century.

DISTANCE *5 miles (8km)*   MINIMUM TIME *1hr 45min*

ASCENT/GRADIENT *130ft (40m)* ▲▲▲   LEVEL OF DIFFICULTY +++

PATHS *Track and field, quiet lanes, ford or bridge, 2 stiles*

LANDSCAPE *Rolling fields, with good views at some points*

SUGGESTED MAP *OS Explorer OL45 The Cotswolds*

START / FINISH *Grid reference: SP 240362*

DOG FRIENDLINESS *Some livestock and some not very encouraging signs*

PARKING *Lay-bys on Todenham's main street, south of village hall*

PUBLIC TOILETS *None en route*

There are cases of so-called 'lost villages' all over England and almost as many theories and explanations for their demise. The principal culprit is often said to be the Black Death, sweeping through the countryside in the 14th century and emptying villages of their inhabitants. However, this is by no means the only possibility and in the case of the Ditchfords there do appear to be other reasons for their disappearance. Ditchford is a name that was widespread in this area (perhaps because of their proximity to the Fosse Way – 'fosse' meaning ditch in Old English). Remnants of this, in the form of the names of houses and farms, are still evident on detailed maps, but of the three villages – Ditchford Frary, Lower Ditchford and Upper Ditchford – there is almost no trace.

Abandonment

A 15th-century witness, a priest from Warwickshire called John Rouse, wrote in 1491 that the Ditchfords had been abandoned during his lifetime. Changes in agricultural practices are thought to be the principal reason for this abandonment. As farming gradually became more efficient there was a disinclination to cultivate the stony soils of the more exposed and windswept upland areas.

At the same time, in the Cotswolds, the wool trade was rapidly supplanting arable farming, as the wolds were given over to sheep. Much of the land was owned by the great abbeys who, deriving a third of their income from wool, turned vast tracts of land over to summer pasture in the uplands and winter pastures on the more sheltered lower slopes. The result was that the villagers, mostly farm labourers who had for centuries depended on access to arable land for their livelihood, lost that access. They simply had to move elsewhere in search of work. Today there are no solid remains of any of the three villages. What you can see, however, is a series of regular rolls and shapes in the land that indicate settlement. Upper Ditchford, which stood on the slope near Neighbrook Farm, is the least obvious but you can see banked enclosures and terraces that probably supported buildings. The site is somewhat clearer in the case of Lower

THE DITCHFORDS

Ditchford, where there are terraces and the site of a manor house and moat. Ditchford Frary has left its name to a nearby farmhouse.

Surviving Village

Todenham survived the rigours of depopluation, and today is a quiet and unspoilt village situated on the edge of the Cotswolds. It's really a long, single road flanked by an assortment of houses and their leafy gardens. The manor house dates from the end of the Georgian period, while the church is worth a visit for its decorated and Perpendicular interior. Its features include a 13th-century font with the names of 18th-century churchwardens inscribed upon it.

WALK 12

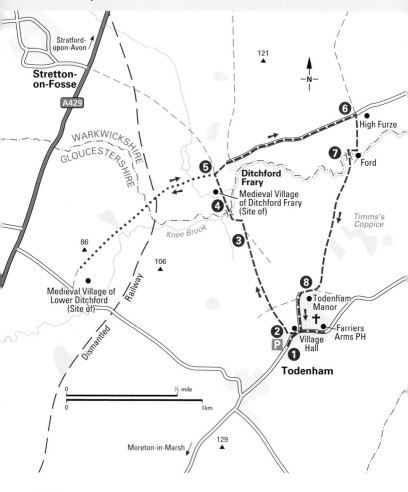

WALK 12 DIRECTIONS

❶ From a lay-by below Todenham village hall walk up towards the hall and turn left just before it. Continue along a gravelled drive between a house (The Retreat) and its garage and the go through solid timber gates.

❷ After 50 paces go right up steps to a bank to a kissing gate. Pass into a field and head straight across. Go through another kissing

THE DITCHFORDS

gate on the far side, into a field of undulations indicating medieval ploughing. Continue on the same line to a stile – cross into the neighbouring field and, staying on its upper part, go straight ahead, in the direction of a large house.

❸ Cross another stile and join a farm track. Where the track goes into a field on the right bear left to pass to the right of a brick ruin, and cross a footbridge to a second footbridge with gates at each end.

❹ Cross this bridge and then go straight ahead, crossing a field (amid the earthworks of the site of Ditchford Frary) with a farmhouse ahead to the right. On the other side go through a field gate, cross another field and pass through a field gate to a farm track.

❺ If you wish to see the site of Lower Ditchford, turn left here on to the metalled track and keep going over the former railway line until you approach a road – the remains are to your left. Then return along the track. Otherwise turn right on the track and pass behind the farmhouse. The track becomes a metalled lane.

❻ After 0.5 mile (800m) just before High Furze farm turn right through a gate into a field. Follow its left margin until it dips down to a ford across Knee Brook. Turn right here and after 70 paces find a bridge on your left.

❼ Cross this ancient stone bridge and head uphill to the faint, grassy track that rises from the ford. By staying on this line, with the brook now to your right, you will come to a gate in the top corner. Go through on to a track that rises between tree lines and copses. After 0.5 mile (800m) you reach a junction opposite an entrance to Todenham Manor.

❽ Turn right here and follow this track as it curves left, around the manor between post and rail fences, and finally brings you back to the village with the village hall on your right. Turn left for the church and the Farriers Arms pub, or turn right to return to your car.

Winchcombe and Sudeley Castle

A rewarding walk above a thriving Cotswold market town and the burial place of Henry's sixth queen — Catherine Parr.

> **DISTANCE** *4 miles (6.4km)* **MINIMUM TIME** *2hrs*
> **ASCENT/GRADIENT** *490ft (150m)* ▲▲▲ **LEVEL OF DIFFICULTY** ✚✚✚
> **PATHS** *Fields and lanes, 13 stiles*
> **LANDSCAPE** *Woodland, hills and town*
> **SUGGESTED MAP** *OS Explorer OL45 The Cotswolds*
> **START / FINISH** *Grid reference: SP 024282*
> **DOG FRIENDLINESS** *On lead (or close control) throughout — much livestock*
> **PARKING** *Free on Abbey Terrace; also car park on Back Lane*
> **PUBLIC TOILETS** *On corner of Vine Street*

At the end of a long drive just outside Winchcombe is a largely 16th-century mansion called Sudeley Castle. The first castle was built here in 1140 and fragments dating from its earlier, more martial days are still much in evidence. Originally little more than a fortified manor house, by the mid-15th century it had acquired a keep and several courtyards. It became a royal castle after the Wars of the Roses before being given to Thomas Seymour, Edward VI's Lord High Admiral. Seymour lived at Sudeley with his wife, Catherine Parr — he was her fourth husband. Seymour was executed for treason. Consequently the castle passed to Catherine's brother, William, but he was executed too. Queen Mary gave the property to Sir John Brydges, the first Lord Chandos. Sudeley Castle was a Royalist stronghold during the Civil War. It was disarmed by the Parliamentarians and left to decay until its purchase by the wealthy Dent brothers in 1863.

Married at Nine Years Old

Catherine Parr, sixth wife of Henry VIII and the only one to outlive him, is buried in Sudeley's chapel. She was born in 1512 into an influential northern family and educated in Henry's court. She was first married at the tender age of nine, but widowed six years later. Back at court, she was at the centre of a group of educated, capable women, using her influence with the King to protect her second husband, Lord Latimer, from the machinations of courtly politics. When Latimer died in 1543, Catherine was left one of the wealthiest and best-connected women in England, and an obvious choice of wife for Henry. She looked after him and his affairs during the years until his death in 1547. Then she quickly married Seymour and moved to Sudeley, where the future Queen Elizabeth was often her companion until Catherine's death in childbirth in 1548.

Winchcombe has a considerable history. In Anglo-Saxon times it was a seat of the Mercian kings and the capital of Winchcombshire until the shire's incorporation into Gloucestershire in the 11th century. It became a significant place of pilgrimage due to the presence of an abbey established in 798 and dedicated to St Kenelm, son of its founder, King Kenulf.

WINCHCOMBE

Grinning Gargoyles

The abbey was razed in the Dissolution, but the town's parish church survived and is a fine example of a 'wool church', financed through income from the medieval wool trade. Of particular interest are the amusing gargoyles that decorate its exterior. They are said to be modelled on real local people. Winchcombe also has two stimulating small museums. It has has also managed to retain many of its shops and other vital local services.

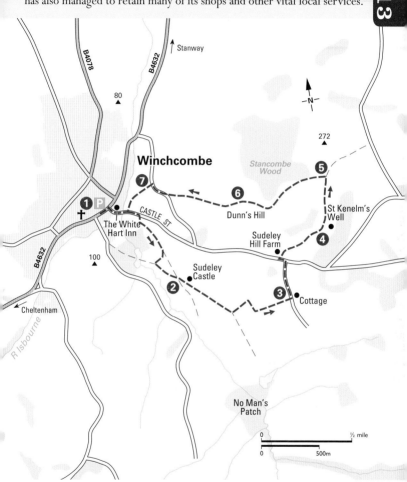

WALK 13 DIRECTIONS

❶ From the parking area on Abbey Terrace in Winchcombe, walk towards the town centre past a Lloyds TSB bank and turn right, down Castle Street. Where it levels out, cross a river bridge and after a few paces bear right to leave the road near the Sudeley Castle Country Cottages and

ascend to a kissing gate. Follow the path through the middle of a long field to a kissing gate. At a track, with the castle visitor centre ahead, turn right for 50 paces, then left through a gate.

❷ Walk between fences, a play fort on the right, to a kissing gate. Follow the left fence past Sudeley Castle, then across its parkland

WALK 13

(guide posts). Over a stile in the far corner turn left and after 25 paces climb another stile and walk alongside the left-hand field boundary, then right at the corner alongside a fence. At the willows go left over stile and walk uphill beside hedging towards a cottage.

3 Through a gate turn left on to a lane and follow this to a junction, turning left. After about 50 paces and just before Sudeley Hill Farm turn right and over a stile. Head half left uphill and over another stile. Over this cross the middle of the field, then bear to the left of a cottage to a stile.

4 Over this you see St Kenelm's Well, a 17th- to 19th-century

building in a fenced enclosure. Pass to the left of this along a track. Cross a stream and go through a gate (or over the stile) and climb half right towards a gate at the right end of woodland.

5 At a woodland fence corner turn left, short of the gate, and go left alongside the fence, over two stiles alongside a small fenced field. Beyond this the path drops, fairly close to the woods on your right, and curves left to a gate. Through this continue alongside the wood, then a line of trees, to a gate and stile in the far corner.

6 Descend half right towards Winchcombe, heading to the furthest corner. Over a stile descend, a fence on your right. At the fence corner continue half right across the field. Through the hedge into the next field continue half left towards a gate. Over the nearby stile cross the field corner to another stile and a footbridge. Half left in the next field head for the gap to the right of a cottage. Through the gate turn right on to a lane, passing a heavily buttressed kitchen garden wall on your left.

7 After about 100yds (91m) turn left through a kissing gate and head across the field towards Winchcombe church tower. Then veer left before the river valley bottom to a kissing gate by a stone cottage. Follow this path to Castle Street and turn right over the river bridge and back into the town centre.

The Sacred Tombs of Belas Knap

A walk from Winchcombe to discover the secrets of one of the best preserved neolithic barrows in the country.

DISTANCE *5 miles (8km)* MINIMUM TIME *2hrs 30min*

ASCENT/GRADIENT *710ft (216m)* ▲▲▲ LEVEL OF DIFFICULTY +++

PATHS *Fields and lanes, 8 stiles*

LANDSCAPE *Wooded escarpment and village*

SUGGESTED MAP *OS Explorer OL45 The Cotswolds*

START / FINISH *Grid reference: SP 024282*

DOG FRIENDLINESS *Pretty good, but livestock in parts*

PARKING *Abbey Terrace or car park on Back Lane, Winchcombe*

PUBLIC TOILETS *On corner of Vine Street*

The Cotswolds are riddled with settlement remains from all eras, including early tombs. Belas Knap (it means beacon hill), a huge green mound in a field overlooking Winchcombe, is one of the most evocative.

Burial Sites

Barrows (often known in Scotland and Wales as cairns) are widespread throughout the country, especially in the south and west of England. The earliest types, neolithic long barrows, were built over a vast time span, between 4000 and 1800 BC. Usually constructed of earth or chalk, they are normally between 98ft and 295ft (30m/90m) long and between 30ft and 98ft (9m/30m) wide. They were used, it is thought, as the burial places of tribal chiefs and their families. Utensils – food vessels for example – were often buried with them in mortuary chambers of wood or of stone, which then, over time, were covered with earth. The burial chamber, containing between six and eight bodies, tended to be at one end of the barrow.

Round Barrows

Round barrows were a feature of the Bronze Age (1800–550 BC). They are much more variable in size and form, but in general they are shaped like bowls, bells or discs and are up to about 20ft (6m) in height and between 12ft and 99ft (4m/30m) in diameter.

Barrows were not a purely prehistoric phenomenon and they continued to be built – albeit only irregularly – by both the Romans and the Saxons (until about AD 750). Once the parish system took hold, however, and as the rites of the Christian Church became established, so the idea of communal earthen burial chambers fell away, to be replaced by permanent buildings dedicated to public worship.

Long Barrows

The long barrow at Belas Knap, dating to approximately 2500 BC, has a false portal (apparently to warn off intruders) of breathtakingly exact dry-stone work. The real entrances to the burial chambers are at the sides. Just who

55

precisely was entombed here is unknown but it is surmised that ancestor worship was widely practised and that the mound was opened many times over the centuries to admit further generations of worthy souls.

Community Project

No doubt the whole community worked at its construction over many months, and maintained it devotedly. It is possible that the barrow became the centrepiece of the settlement, seen as a tangible link with the past – certainly it would have been a significant presence on the treeless wolds. Thirty-eight skeletons have been found inside the tomb, which is constructed of slabs of limestone, covered in turf.

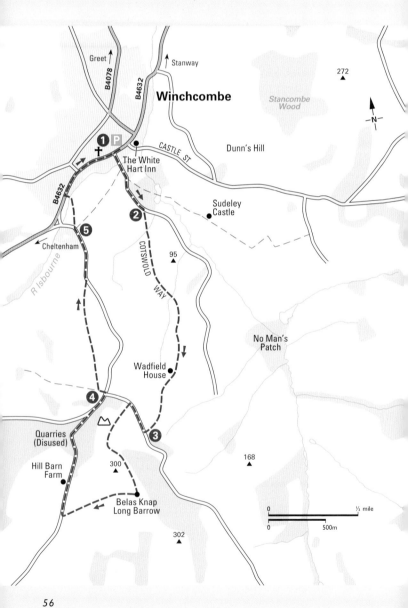

WALK 14 DIRECTIONS

❶ From Abbey Terrace, walk along the main street in the direction of Cheltenham. Shortly turn left down Vineyard Street, towards Sudeley Castle. Walk down the street flanked by pretty cottages, cross a bridge and come to the entrance to the castle, near a lodge. Stay on the road as it bears right and, after 300yds (274m), go through a kissing gate on the right.

❷ Go half left to a stile and cross two further fields via a stile and footbridge on the same line. In the far corner of the third field, cross a footbridge, with stiles at each end, to a field and follow its right-hand margin to a stile on the right. Go over, turn left and follow the field margin as it rises. Cross a footbridge and stile, pass Wadfield House and walk on a track, passing to the right of a pair of cottages, to a road.

❸ Turn right. After 400yds (366m) turn left at a stile on to a steep path among trees. Go

through a field kissing gate and turn left to follow its north and east margin to the top. Go through a kissing gate and turn left. Eventually go through another kissing gate to arrive at Belas Knap over a stone stile. Leave the site via another stone stile on the opposite side and walk ahead until you come to a track. Turn right and descend for 0.5 mile (800m) to a road junction at a hairpin bend.

❹ Go left through a gate into a field and descend towards a cricket pitch to a kissing gate at the bottom. Turn right along a track. At the road gate turn left. After 500yds (457m) go right through a kissing gate into a field.

❺ Go half left to willow trees and a kissing gate and footbridge. Beyond, go up a path to the road. Turn right and make your way back to Abbey Terrace.

HAILES ABBEY

Thomas Cromwell and Hailes Abbey

How an important abbey was destroyed by a King's Commissioner.

WALK 15

DISTANCE 5 miles (8km)	**MINIMUM TIME** 2hrs
ASCENT/GRADIENT 605ft (185m) ▲▲▲	**LEVEL OF DIFFICULTY** +++

PATHS Fields, tracks, farmyard and lanes, 4 stiles

LANDSCAPE Wide views, rolling wolds and villages

SUGGESTED MAP OS Explorer OL45 The Cotswolds

START / FINISH Grid reference: SP 051302

DOG FRIENDLINESS Mostly on lead – a lot of livestock in fields

PARKING Beside Hailes church

PUBLIC TOILETS None en route

In the decade from 1536 to 1547 just about every English religious institution that was not a parish church was either closed or destroyed – this was the Dissolution, Henry VIII's draconian policy to force the old Church to give up its wealth. The smaller monasteries went first, then the larger ones and finally the colleges and chantries. All their lands and tithes became Crown property. Much of them were sold off to laypeople, usually local landowners. The Church as a parish institution was considerably strengthened as a result of the Dissolution, but at the expense of the wider religious life. The suppression of the chantries and guilds, for example, meant many people were deprived of a local place of worship.

Hailes Abbey

Hailes Abbey was one of the most powerful Cistercian monasteries in the country, owning 13,000 acres (5,265ha) and 8,000 sheep. It was a particular target for reformers. In 1270 Edmund, Earl of Cornwall, the son of its founder, had given the monastery a phial supposed to contain the blood of Christ. Thomas Cromwell was the King's Commissioner responsible for seeing to the closure of the monasteries. He is reputed to have surveyed the destruction of the monastery from a vantage point near Beckbury Camp. There is still a fine view of the abbey from here, as you should find as you pass Point ❺ on this walk. According to Hugh Latimer of Worcester, who had been working with him, Cromwell also spent an afternoon in 1539 examining the so-called 'blood'. Cromwell concluded that it was nothing more than an 'unctuous gum and compound of many things'. Once the valuables had been removed, local people took what was left.

The monastery lands were disposed of in a typical manner. First they were confiscated by the Crown and then sold to a speculator who sold the land on in lots. In about 1600 the site of the abbey was bought by Sir John Tracy, the builder of Stanway House. The monks were dispersed: a few managed to secure positions as part of the parish clergy, while others took up posts with the cathedrals at Bristol and Gloucester. Others returned to the laity.

Charming Remains

Hailes church is all that remains of the village of Hailes. It predates the abbey and survived the Dissolution, perhaps because it had been a parish church and was not directly linked to the neighbouring monastery. It is a church of real charm, sadly ignored by the many visitors to the monastery's ruins. Although very small, it has several special features, including a panelled chancel – floored with tiles from the monastery – and a nave with 14th-century wall paintings. Didbrook church also survived the upheavals. Built in Perpendicular style, it was rebuilt in 1475 by the Abbot of Hailes, following damage caused by Lancastrian soldiers after the Battle of Tewkesbury.

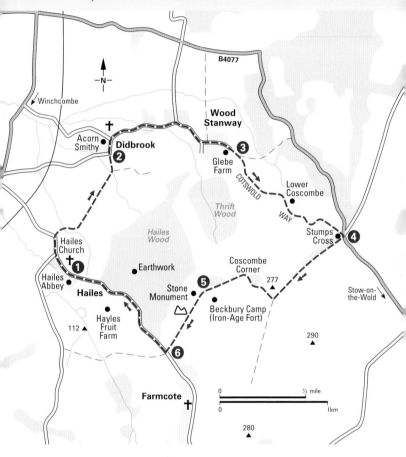

WALK 15 DIRECTIONS

❶ From Hailes church turn right and follow the lane to a T-junction. Turn right here and after 200yds (183m) turn right again on to a footpath through a gate. Walk aross an area of concrete, go over a stile next to a gate and

follow a track as it goes right and left, turning at an old oak tree, eventually becoming a grassy path beside a field. Go over a stile, followed by a stile and footbridge. After about 75yds (69m) turn left, through a gate, and cross a field alongside the right-hand hedge to reach a gate at a road.

WALK 15

❷ Turn right and follow the road as it meanders through the pretty village of Didbrook then a stretch of countryside. At a junction turn right for Wood Stanway. Walk through this village, bearing left at a cherry tree on a grass island, into the yard of Glebe Farm.

❸ Ignore a bridleway sign and gate on the left and at a gate go on to a track on the left of a field and walk ahead, looking for a gate on the left. You are now on the Cotswold Way, well marked by arrows with a white dot or acorn. Cross into a field and go half right, keeping to the left of some electricity poles, to a gate in a hedge. Bear half left across the next field, heading towards farm buildings. Through a gate turn sharp right, up the slope, (guide posts), to a gate on your right. Through this turn immediately left up the field to a guide post. Go through a gate. Follow the footpath as it wends its way gently up the slope. At the top walk along the crest, with a dry stone wall to your right, to a reach gate at a road.

❹ Turn right and right again through a gate to a track. Follow this for 0.5 mile (800m), passing through a gate, until at the top (just before some trees), you turn right to follow another track for 50yds (46m). Turn left through a gate into a field and turn sharp right to follow the perimeter of

the field as it goes left and passes through a gate beside the ramparts of an Iron Age fort, Beckbury Camp. Continue ahead to pass through another gate which leads to a stone monument with a niche. According to local lore, from here Thomas Cromwell watched the destruction of Hailes Abbey in 1539.

❺ Turn right to follow a steep path down through the trees. At the bottom go straight across down the field to a gate. Pass through, continue down to another gate and, in the field beyond, head down to a stile beside a signpost.

❻ Over this turn right down a lane, all the way to a road. To the left is Hayles Fruit Farm with its café. Continue ahead along the road to return to Hailes Abbey and the start point by the church.

Around Cutsdean and Ford

The origins of the Cotswolds, once the focus of England's most valued export.

DISTANCE 6 miles (9.7km)   **MINIMUM TIME** 2hrs 30min

ASCENT/GRADIENT 265ft (80m) ▲▲▲   **LEVEL OF DIFFICULTY** ✦✦✦

PATHS Tracks, fields and lane, 5 stiles

LANDSCAPE Open wold, farmland, village

SUGGESTED MAP OS Explorer OL45 The Cotswolds

START / FINISH Grid reference: SP 088302

DOG FRIENDLINESS Best on leads – plenty of livestock, including horses

PARKING Cutsdean village street

PUBLIC TOILETS None en route

Cutsdean can claim to be the centre of the Cotswolds, according to one theory about the origin of the name 'cotswold'. Today it is nothing more than a small, pretty village on the high, voluptuous wolds above the beginnings of the River Windrush. However, it may once have been the seat of an Anglo-Saxon chief by the name of 'Cod'. His domain would have been his 'dene' and the hilly region in which his domain lay, his 'wolds'. This is plausible, even if there is no verifiable record of a King Cod. Another explanation concerns the sheep that still graze many hillsides in the Cotswolds, a 'cot' referring to a sheep fold and 'wolds' being the hills that support them. (In Old English a 'cot' is a small dwelling or cottage.)

Lamb's Wool to Lion's Wool

Whatever the truth of the matter, the sheep remain, even if the species that in the Middle Ages produced the finest wool in Europe dwindled to the point of extinction. The ancestors of the 'Cotswold Lion' probably arrived with the Romans, who valued the sheeps' milk and their long, dense wool. The nature of the Cotswolds was perfect for these sheep: the limestone soil produces a calcium-rich diet, good for strong bone growth; and the open, wind-blasted wolds suited this heavy-fleeced breed, able to graze all year long on herbs and grasses. The hills teemed with Cotswold sheep; at one point the Cotswold wool trade accounted for half of England's income.

Distinctive Forelock

It is believed that the medieval Cotswold sheep differed a little from its modern counterpart. Its coat was undoubtedly long and lustrous, but it may have been slightly shorter than that of its descendants. It was the distinctive forelock and the whiteness of its fleece that inspired the nickname, Cotswold Lion, characteristics that persist in the modern sheep.

Under Threat

Why, then, did the fortunes of this miraculous animal plummet? To some extent this is a misconception, since serious decline occurred only with the

CUTSDEAN

move to arable farming in the Cotswolds in the mid-20th century. Demand
for the wool was strong in the 18th and 19th centuries and the Cotswold
was also prized for its meat and its cross-breeding potential. However, the
market for long-stapled wool began to decline in favour of finer wool, and
crop growing became more attractive to local farmers. Incredibly, by the
1960s, there remained only some 200 animals. Suddenly, it was clear that a
living piece of English history was on the verge of extinction. The Cotswold
Breed Society was reconvened and steps were taken to ensure the sheep's
survival. Farmers have since rediscovered the animal's many qualities, and
it is no longer quite such a rare sight on the wolds.

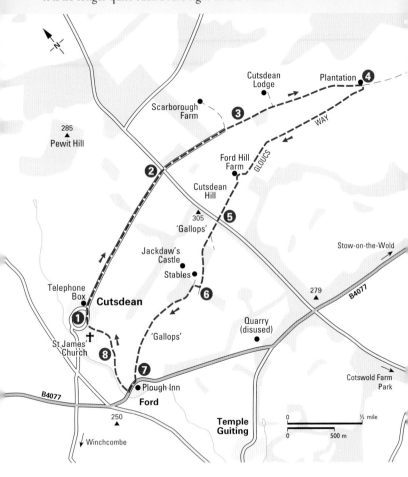

WALK 16 DIRECTIONS

❶ With the Church of St James
to your right-hand side and, after
a few paces, a telephone box away
in a lane to your left, walk out
of the village of Cutsdean past
Stoneley. Continue uphill on this
straight country road for just over

a mile (1.6km), until you come to
a T-junction with another road.

❷ Cross this to enter another
lane past a 'No Through Road'
sign, at the margin of woodland.
Beyond a second wood, where the
track veers left towards a house,
go straight on along a stony track.

3 Eventually you come to a gate. Through this continue along the track, initially a wood to your right, to another gate, ignoring a footpath to the left at the brow of the hill. Through the gate the path has a stone wall on the left for a field and a half, the path then goes quarter right over the brow of a slope to head for a plantation.

4 Emerging beyond the plantation turn immediately right at a track junction and right again, the plantation now on your right. Follow this track for 1.5 miles (2.4km), passing through Ford Hill Farm, all the way to a road.

5 Across the road go through a gate, signed 'Jackdaw's Castle' and follow a tarmac lane which runs to the left of a 'gallops' used for training racehorses. Keep straight on where the track veers left into a neighbouring field.

6 Soon after passing the stables of Jackdaw's Castle across to your right, you need to turn sharp right at a footpath sign across the gallops area (watch out for

horses) to join a tarmac track, where you turn left. The track descends gently for just under a mile (1.6km), the gallops and greensward to your left. Keep descending until you are near the bottom, at the beginning of a village. This is Ford: if you walk into the village you will see the welcoming Plough Inn directly in front of you.

7 Otherwise turn right and, at a bend, turn right again to cross a car parking area to a stile. Over this walk along a grassy path, a post and rail fence to your right, a stream in a steep valley to your left, soon passing through a gate. The path leaves the fence and then descends through the copse to a stile.

8 Cross the stile into a field and then go half right across it. Go down a bank, across a rivulet (possibly dried up in summertime) and up the bank on the other side to a stile. Cross into a field and turn left along the side of the field towards Cutsdean. Pass to the right of the church, which sits back across a wall to your left. At the edge of the village come to a stile: cross this to join a track. After 25 paces emerge on to the main street through the village and your starting point.

Empires and Poets at Adlestrop and Daylesford

Embracing the legacies of Warren Hastings and the poet Edward Thomas.

DISTANCE 5 miles (8km)	**MINIMUM TIME** 2hrs 15min
ASCENT/GRADIENT 230ft (70m) ▲▲▲	**LEVEL OF DIFFICULTY** +++

PATHS Track, field and road, 1 stile

LANDSCAPE Rolling fields, woodland and villages

SUGGESTED MAP OS Explorer OL45 The Cotswolds

START / FINISH Grid reference: SP 242272

DOG FRIENDLINESS Some livestock but some open areas and quiet lanes

PARKING Car park (donations requested) outside village hall

PUBLIC TOILETS None en route

Warren Hastings is a name that is simultaneously familiar and elusive; his role, however, in the making of the British Empire, was paramount. Born in the nearby village of Churchill, in 1732, he spent much of his childhood in Daylesford, where his grandfather was rector. When debt forced the sale of the manor, Hastings was sent to London for a career in commerce. He joined the East India Company, which was de facto ruler of India, and by 1773 he had attained the rank of Governor-General of Bengal, with the specific remit of cleaning up the corruption that was rife among the British and Indian ruling classes. His draconian methods were often resented but his determination and guile were effective. That India became the fulcrum of the British Empire was largely due to his work. Upon his return to England, he used his savings to repurchase Daylesford, where he died in 1818. The years before his death were bitter. A change in attitude to colonialist methods meant that Hastings was impeached for corruption. The seven year trial bankrupted him and ruined his health, although he was eventually vindicated and made Privy Councillor to George III.

Spacious Parkland

Daylesford House was rebuilt by Warren Hastings to the design of the architect Samuel Cockerell, who had been a colleague at the East India Company. The building is in a classical style with Moorish features. The parkland around Daylesford House was laid out in 1787 by the landscape gardener Humphrey Repton in the spacious style of the day, made popular by Lancelot 'Capability' Brown. The village grew out of a need for cottages for estate workers. Similarly, Daylesford church was rebuilt by Hastings in 1816 as a place of worship for the estate workers. By 1860 the congregation had outgrown the church, so it was redesigned to accommodate it. Inside there are monuments to the Hastings family, while Warren Hastings' tomb lies outside the east window.

If Hastings represents the British Empire at its strongest then, in Adlestrop, you will find echoes of the changing world which signalled its decline. This characteristically rural small village, has come to be associated

ADLESTROP

with one of the best-known poems in English, written by the war poet, Edward Thomas (1878–1917). Called simply *Adlestrop*, the poem captures a single moment as a train halts briefly at the village's station. Its haunting evocation of the drowsy silence of a hot summer day is all the more poignant when it is borne in mind that Thomas was killed by an exploding shell at Ronville near Arras in April 1917. Though trains still run on the line, the station was closed in 1964. You'll find the old station sign now decorates a bus shelter and the old station bench has the poem inscribed upon it.

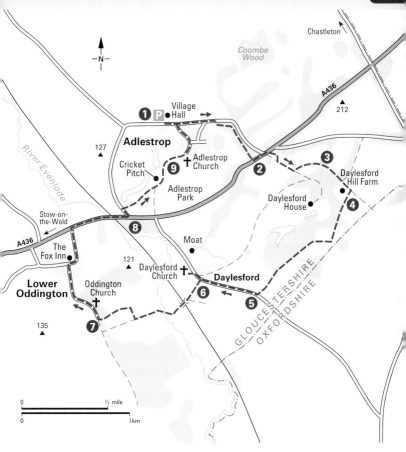

WALK 17 DIRECTIONS

1 From the car park outside the village hall turn left along the road. Pass a road on the right, the bus shelter bearing the Adlestrop sign, and some houses. Some 200yds (183m) after another road, turn right over a stile. Follow a woodland path to the left. Continue on this path until it meets a gate at a road.

2 Cross the road with care and turn left along the verge. Before a road on the right and after West Lodge turn right through a wooden gate on to a path in the Daylesford Estate. The path curves left to a post and rail fence. Turn right alongside it as it curves to the drive. Turn left on to the drive, flanked by poplar trees, and after 100 paces turn left between post and rail fences.

65

❸ Follow these to cross a bridge and follow a tree-lined avenue towards buildings. Traverse the farmyard and then turn right at Hill Farm Cottage, passing the estate office.

❹ Walk along the drive between paddocks, soon following the estate wall. Pass the garden offices' gate and, as it goes sharp right, stay on the drive, reaching a road. Turn right at a gate.

❺ Walk along the road, with the estate on your right, until you come to Daylesford estate village. Opposite the drive to Daylesford House is a shaded footpath leading to Daylesford church. After visiting the church, return to the road, turn right and retrace your steps and 95 paces beyond the phone box, turn right through a kissing gate.

❻ Cross this field to a gate. Turn right on to a track and cross a

railway footbridge. Curve along the track through two field gates to cross an iron lattice-sided footbridge over the stream. Almost immediately turn right off the track, then left by the hedge to walk parallel to the track. At the end of the field turn left through a gate back onto the track, through a gate and then right, beyond the hedge. The path follows two sides of the field to a gate into a copse in the far corner.

❼ At a track through the trees turn right and pass Oddington church. Continue, now on tarmac, to a junction in the village and turn right. Pass the Fox Inn and go to another junction. Turn right and walk on the pavement. Where it ends, cross the road carefully to the pavement opposite.

❽ Beyond the railway bridge, turn left along the Adlestrop road and turn immediately right through two kissing gates. Descend through Adlestrop Park to skirt to the right of the cricket pitch and head for a kissing gate to its right, in a tree gap.

❾ Follow the track through a kissing gate and past Adlestrop church. At the next junction turn left through the village until you reach the bus stop. Turn left here to return to the car park at the start of the walk.

Adlestrop to Chastleton

From a timeless village to an age-old house.

DISTANCE *4 miles (6.4km)* MINIMUM TIME *2hrs*
ASCENT/GRADIENT *427ft (130m)* ▲▲▲ LEVEL OF DIFFICULTY **+++**
PATHS *Meadows, lanes, woodland, 7 stiles*
LANDSCAPE *Low rolling hills north of Chipping Norton*
SUGGESTED MAP *OS Explorer OL45 The Cotswolds*
START / FINISH *Grid reference: SP 242272*
DOG FRIENDLINESS *Some road walking; not permitted in Chastleton House*
PARKING *Car park (donations requested) beside village hall, Adlestrop*
PUBLIC TOILETS *None en route*

The walk starts in the sleepy village of Adlestrop. It was not always so quiet, for trains used to stop here. The poet Edward Thomas (1878–1917) wrote a wistful verse in which he recalled stopping here unexpectedly on the express train, apparently in the middle of nowhere, and listening to the birdsong (See Walk 17). Set in deep, lush countryside, Adlestrop still feels well off the beaten track. Its houses are a pleasing harmony of old and new, stone roofs alternating with thatch, and cottage gardens to die for.

Chastleton House

One of the finest Jacobean mansions in England, Chastleton House stands on the hillside above its village, aloof and self-contained. The house has a magical stillness about it. It was built between 1603 and 1618 by a local wool merchant, Walter Jones, on land purchased from Robert Catesby, one of the Gunpowder plotters.

Time-worn Perfection

Its handsome grey stone frontage, with its tall windows and symmetrical gables and staircase towers, is seen clearly from the road. If you want to see inside, however, you are urged to book ahead, for opening hours and numbers are strictly limited. Chastleton is no grand showplace and, since its acquisition in 1991, the National Trust has been careful to conserve it in its peaceful, time-worn perfection, rather than attempt to restore it to some former glory. There is a panelled hall, an ornate great chamber and a vast long gallery, with plastered ceiling, on the top floor looks out over the gardens. Much of the furniture is original, and chambers are richly furnished with embroideries, quilts and tapestries.

Chastleton may have led a quiet life, but hardly a dull one. A secret room above the parlour was used to hide a fugitive in the Civil War. Arthur Jones was a Royalist, and had fought for the King – and lost – at the Battle of Worcester in 1651. He fled to his father's house at Chastleton and was forced into the hiding place when a party of soldiers arrived in hot pursuit. Arthur's wife, Sarah, was obliged to put them up for the night. This

CHASTLETON

WALK 18

resourceful woman laced their ale with laudanum and, while his pursuers snored, Arthur made his escape. He was able to return at the Restoration and planted an oak in the grounds to celebrate his narrow escape.

Croquet on the Lawn

The formal gardens at Chastleton are contemporary with the house. It is sometimes claimed that croquet was invented here. The game had been around for centuries, but was introduced to England in 1852. The rules of the game were set out for the first time here at Chastleton in 1865.

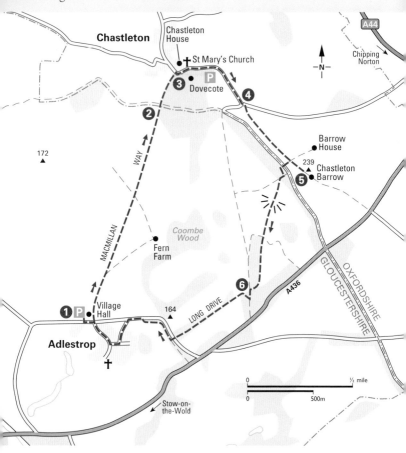

WALK 18 DIRECTIONS

1 From the car park in Adlestrop turn left on to the road and left again up a broad track, passing stables, and signposted 'Macmillan Way'. Climb a stile by a gate and enter a meadow. Bear left (yellow waymarker). Walk up the field, with Fern Farm up to your right. Cross a stile in the top left

corner and continue up the fence. Soon cross a stile to your left and continue up the same line, passing a bulging oak tree on your right. Cross another stile and continue straight ahead up the field. The hill gets steeper.

2 Cross a stile by a wooden gate and walk up through the line of trees. Continue straight across the next field. Go over the crest of the hill and through an iron gate, into the Chastleton Estate. Continue straight ahead up an avenue of trees. Go through two gates to reach the road.

❸ Turn right and walk along the road, passing Chastleton House on your left, then St Mary's Church. Pass the arcaded dovecote on the right. Stay on the road, which bends up right, and pass a car park on your right.

WHILE YOU'RE THERE

The walk offers excellent views across to the busy market town of Stow-on-the-Wold, reached along the A436. Perched on the very edge of the wolds, it is known to catch any blast of wind, and can be icy in winter – hence the local saying, 'Stow-on-the-Wold, where the wind blows cold'. This is antique-hunter's heaven, however, and there's a steady flow of visitors to explore the shops whatever the season.

WHAT TO LOOK OUT FOR

Walking into the green ring of Chastleton Barrow is an eerie experience. Surrounded by a bank or rampart planted with trees, it clearly functioned once as a defensive site, most probably in the Iron Age. An ancient track linked the camp with the Rollright Stones (See Walk 22). This wide grassy amphitheatre on the hilltop is now used to hold cattle.

❹ Where the road bends sharply right, turn left into a private road. Cross a cattle grid and immediately turn right. Go through a gate and take the bridleway diagonally left up the field, parallel with the road. On a level with Barrow House farm, go through a small gate, cross the drive and take the left of two gates opposite. Go through two more gates to enter the tree circle of Chastleton Barrow.

❺ When you have seen the barrow, retrace your route to the drive and turn left. At the road cross over and go through the gate opposite. Bear left through the trees and follow the path, which leads diagonally right across the field, with views to Stow-on-the-Wold. Keep straight on down, passing some barns to your left.

Cross a track and walk ahead down the edge of woodland. At the bottom corner bear right into the woods. Follow the winding path through a gap and emerge at a field.

❻ Turn left along the track. Turn right before you reach the gateway, and walk down the edge of the field. Go through a gate into the Long Drive. Follow this path through the trees and emerge via a stile on to the road. Cross over, go through a gateway on the other side and soon turn right along a narrow footpath. Follow this through the trees; bear right, cross a stile and turn left along the road. Take the first turning left and walk through Adlestrop village, keeping right to return to the car park and the start of the walk.

WHERE TO EAT AND DRINK

The venerable villages of Lower Oddington and Upper Oddington offer an appealing diversion on your way to Stow-on-the-Wold and are served by two good pubs. The Fox Inn at Lower Oddington is set opposite a beautiful little manor house. Continue through the villages to reach the Horse and Groom at Upper Oddington, which has the bonus of a big car park behind.

A Ghostly Trail Around Prestbury

A gentle ramble around this unassuming old village which claims to be one of Britain's most haunted.

DISTANCE 3 miles (4.8km) **MINIMUM TIME** 1hr 30min

ASCENT/GRADIENT 100ft (30m) ▲▲▲ **LEVEL OF DIFFICULTY** ✦✦✦

PATHS Fields (could be muddy in places) and pavement, 8 stiles

LANDSCAPE Woodland, hills and villages

SUGGESTED MAP OS Explorer 179 Gloucester, Cheltenham & Stroud

START / FINISH Grid reference: SO 972239

DOG FRIENDLINESS Lead necessary as some fields stocked with farm animals; some stiles have dog slots

PARKING Free car park near war memorial

PUBLIC TOILETS None en route

The village of Prestbury, on the north-east fringe of Cheltenham, is reputedly the second most haunted village in England, with The Burgage its oldest and most haunted street. The largest building along it is Prestbury House, now a hotel. During the Civil War it was occupied by Parliamentary troops. Expecting Royalists camped on Cleeve Hill to send a messenger to Gloucester, they laid a trap. A rope was stretched across The Burgage. When the Cavalier rode through the village, he snagged on the rope and was catapulted from his mount. No doubt relieved of his despatches and interrogated, the unfortunate rider was then executed. A skeleton discovered near by in the 19th century is thought to be his. It is said that the sound of hooves can often be heard here, as well as a horse's snorting and stamping.

Exercise and Exorcism

More paranormal activity has been experienced in the hotel grounds, where they meet Mill Street. Here there have been sightings of rowdy parties of people in Regency dress. On this site, it turns out, there was once a fashionable meeting place, called the Grotto. It was where the local gentry would take their ease. By the time of its closure, in 1859, it had become known as a place of ill-repute.

Spectral abbots are regularly seen in Prestbury. The Black Abbot used to walk the aisle of St Mary's Church but, since his exorcism, he prefers the churchyard – a vicar came across him here, seated on a tombstone. The Abbot has also been spotted in the early morning near the Plough Inn on Mill Street. In fact, there have been sightings of the Black Abbot almost everywhere in the village. Perhaps this may be explained by the fact that the Bishops of Hereford owned a palace here from the 12th century, while the Prior of Llanthony lived in the priory close to the church. There are several other haunted places you will come across in the village. At Sundial Cottage, in The Burgage, a lovelorn girl plays the spinet; the Three Queens house in Deep Street had to be exorcised; there are three stone cottages

PRESTBURY

next to Three Queens, the middle one of which is haunted by soldiers from the Civil War, and the third of which is haunted by the Black Abbot. And another abbot (or perhaps the same one) with 'an unpleasant leer', is said to haunt Morningside House, next to the car park.

There is more to the village than ghosts, however. The manor of Prestbury, belonging to the Bishop of Hereford, was established by 899. Remains of the moated hall can still be found on Spring Lane, close to Cheltenham racecourse. The village is closely associated with the jockey Fred Archer, as a plaque on the King's Arms testifies, while the cricketer Charlie Parker, who played for England, was also born here.

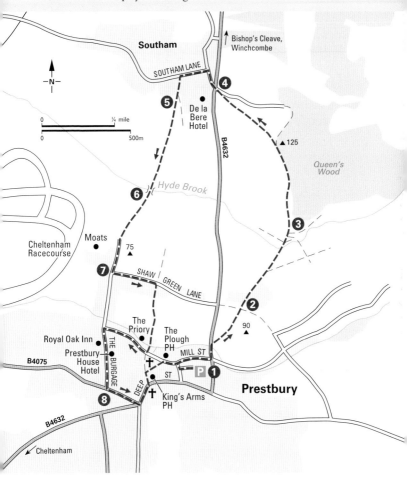

WALK 19 DIRECTIONS

1 Leave the car park, turn right into The Bank and right again into Mill Street. At the main road turn left. After 100yds (91m) cross the road to a stile. Go into a field and go diagonally left to another stile.

2 Cross this and follow the track that is ahead of you and slightly to your left. Where it goes right, cross a stile in front of you. Cross a field heading slightly to the right, to another stile. Go over this into a field and head for Queen's Wood in front of you.

3 Stay to the left of the woods. Eventually cross a track via two stiles and enter another field. Where the woods sweep uphill, keep straight on to drop through a field with old oak trees to a stile in the corner by the main road.

4 Ahead of you are the medieval buildings of the Hotel De La Bere. Cross the road and turn right. Follow the pavement as it bears left into Southam Lane. After 200yds (183m) turn left along a track to a gate. Go through this and a kissing gate to a field.

WHERE TO EAT AND DRINK

There are several pubs to choose from. The King's Arms welcomes children, the Royal Oak Inn also serves lunches and The Plough, on Mill Street, is a very fine old pub with a flagstone floor and a gorgeous garden. Prestbury House Hotel offers an excellent light lunch or dinner in a more formal setting.

5 Head across, bearing slightly right towards an oak tree, with the De La Bere on your left. Follow an obvious path across a series of paddocks and fields via stiles and gates, the path bypassing many of the kissing gates. Finally, at a kissing gate amid bushes in a corner, cross on to a track and follow this as it leads, via a low stile, to a footbridge and gate.

6 Cross and continue straight ahead into a field with a hedge on your right. Go over the brow of the slope through a kissing gate and down to a gate in the hedge to your right. Go through a kissing gate at the corner of the field to a track and follow this to a road.

7 Turn left along Shaw Green Lane. After about 400yds (366m)

WHILE YOU'RE THERE

Cheltenham, of which Prestbury is really a suburb, is a very handsome town and definitely worth a visit. It has fine Regency and Georgian architecture, as well as two excellent small museums, one in the birthplace of composer Gustav Holst (1874–1934), the other with features devoted to the arctic explorer Edward Wilson, and to the Arts and Crafts Movement.

turn right along a footpath passing between houses just past No 34. Eventually this will bring you out on to Mill Street, opposite the church. Turn right, to walk past the Priory and the brick wall that marks the site of the haunted Grotto, until you come to The Burgage. Turn left here, passing the Royal Oak Inn, Prestbury House Hotel and Sundial Cottage.

8 At the junction with Tatchley Lane turn left and then left again at mini-roundabouts into Deep Street, passing the Three Queens and the trio of stone cottages. Just before the King's Arms turn left on a footpath leading to the church. Turn right just before the church and pass through the churchyard to return to Mill Street, opposite The Plough. Turn right and then right again and return to the car park at the start.

WHAT TO LOOK OUT FOR

Don't forget that you are very close to one of Europe's greatest racecourses. As you walk across the fields towards Queen's Wood, you will have some wonderful views across the racecourse to Cheltenham. The Hotel De La Bere is a striking Elizabethan mansion that was once the home of Lord Ellenborough, a former Governor-General of India.

Guiting Power to the People

A gentle ramble in quintessential Gloucestershire, from a typical village with an atypical place-name and atypical ownership.

DISTANCE 6 miles (9.7km)   **MINIMUM TIME** 2hrs

ASCENT/GRADIENT 295ft (90m) ▲▲▲   **LEVEL OF DIFFICULTY** ✦✦✦

PATHS Fields, tracks and country lanes, 7 stiles

LANDSCAPE Woodland, hills and village

SUGGESTED MAP OS Explorer OL45 The Cotswolds

START / FINISH Grid reference: SP 094246

DOG FRIENDLINESS Fairly clear of livestock but many horses on roads

PARKING Car park outside village hall (small fee)

PUBLIC TOILETS None en route

It is remarkable how much detailed history is available about English villages, even ones, like Guiting Power, that are distinguished only by their comeliness. Looking from the village green, surrounded by stone cottages, with its church and secluded manor house, it is easy to imagine that very little has changed here in 1,000 years.

What's in a Name?

The eccentric name comes from the Saxon word 'gyte-ing', or torrent, and indeed the name was given not only to Guiting Power but also to neighbouring Temple Guiting, which in the 12th century was owned by the Knights Templars. Guiting Power though, was named after the pre-eminent local family of the 13th century, the Le Poers.

Over the years the village was variously known as Gything, Getinge, Gettinges Poer, Guyting Poher, Nether Guiting and Lower Guiting. Its current name and spelling date only from 1937. In 1086, the Domesday Book noted that there were 'four villagers, three Frenchmen, two riding men, and a priest with two small-holders'. Just under 100 years later the first recorded English fulling mill was in operation at the nearby hamlet of Barton to the north-east. In 1330 permission was given for a weekly market to be held at Guiting Power, which may explain the current arrangement of the houses about the green. Guiting had its share of the prosperity derived from the 15th-century wool trade, as the addition of the little tower to the church testifies.

Slow to Catch Up

And yet, in other ways, history was slow to catch up with small villages like Guiting. Its farmland, for example, was enclosed only in 1798, allowing small landowners such as a tailor called John Williams, who owned 12 acres (4.86ha) in the form of medieval strips scattered throughout the parish, to finally consolidate their possessions. Local rights of way were enshrined in law at this time. By the end of the 19th century the rural depression had reduced the population to 431, and it continued to decline throughout the

73

GUITING POWER

20th century. Nonetheless, it is recorded that apart from public houses (there were at least four), there were two grocers, two bakers, two tailors, two carpenters, two policemen and a blacksmith.

Local Village for Local People

There are still two pubs in Guiting Power but everything else, apart from the post office and a single grocery store, has disappeared. The village is unusual in that it hasn't succumbed to the inflationary effects of second homeowners from the cities pushing local housing beyond the reach of existing locals. Much of this is down to the far-sightedness of Moya Davidson, a resident in the 1930s, who purchased cottages to be rented out locally. Today these are managed by the Guiting Manor Amenity Trust. It has meant that younger people are able to stay in the village to live and work and there still a few families here who can trace their roots back in Guiting Power for several generations.

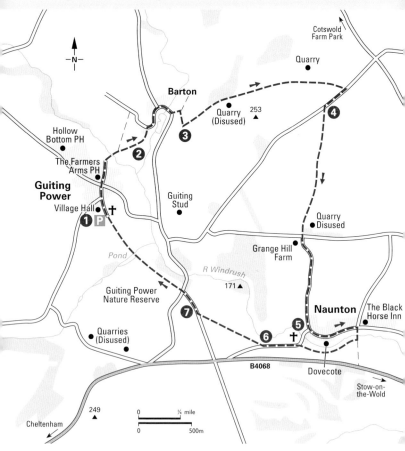

WALK 20 DIRECTIONS

❶ From the village hall car park walk down the road to the village green. Cross the road to walk down a lane, passing the Guiting Manor Amenity Trust Estate Office on the right. At the bottom go through a kissing gate into a field and turn right on to a path alongside a stream. Through a gate and over a footbridge, the path climbs towards a kissing gate. Don't cross the one in front of you but clamber over the one to your right into a field.

2 Turn left and walk straight across this field to another stile. Cross this and two more to pass a farmhouse in Barton village. Follow the lane down to a larger road and turn right. Cross a bridge and turn left up a track and, after 100yds (91m), turn right up another track.

3 After 140 paces bear left and walk along this track for about a mile (1.6km), until you reach another road passing a working quarry. Turn right, walk along here for about 250yds (229m) and turn left on to a stony track.

4 Follow this to a road, passing a quarry as you go. Cross the road and enter a lane descending past Grange Hill Farm. This quiet lane will bring you all the way into the village of Naunton.

5 At the junction turn left and walk along the village street for 500yds (455m) to The Black Horse Inn. Just before it turn right into Close Hill, a narrow lane. Over a bridge turn right to cross a stone slab stile to walk alongside the stream, the young River Windrush. Go over another stile and through two gates. The path becomes a village lane emerging near Naunton church. Turning left, follow the lane up out of the village.

6 After 0.25 mile (400m), through a kissing gate, turn right into a field. Turn left, walk to a stile and go into the next field. Cross this field, enter the next one and follow the path to the right of a wood to a gate at the road.

7 Turn right along the road and continue to a junction at the bottom. Cross the road to enter a field via a gate and walk straight across, aiming to the left of Guiting Power church. At the end go through a kissing gate and down some steps to pass to the right of a pond. Through a kissing gate walk across the next field and then through a kissing gate to walk to the left of the church via two further kissing gates and return to the start.

Churchill and Cornwell

*A walk linking two intriguing villages
on the D'Arcy Dalton Way.*

DISTANCE 5.5 miles (8.8km)	**MINIMUM TIME** 2hrs 30min
ASCENT/GRADIENT 459ft (140m) ▲▲▲	**LEVEL OF DIFFICULTY** ✦✦✦

PATHS Open farmland, village lanes, quiet roads, 5 stiles

LANDSCAPE Broad, open valley once used by a railway line

SUGGESTED MAP OS Explorer OL45 The Cotswolds

START / FINISH Grid reference: SP 270271

DOG FRIENDLINESS Some road walking, otherwise good

PARKING Lay-by beside phone box at Cornwell

PUBLIC TOILETS None en route

There's a slightly theatrical air about Cornwell. It huddles on one side of a small valley, smugly holding on to its secrets, for, as part of the Cornwell Manor Estate, it is private and inaccessible. You may look, but not touch. The manor itself, where owner Peter Ward and his family live today, is carefully screened from prying eyes, except for the lovely stone front, which boldly faces up to the road from behind its high wrought iron gate.

Cornwell

Cornwell's best known secret is that it was thoroughly remodelled just before the Second World War by Clough Williams-Ellis (1883–1978). Born in Northamptonshire, Williams-Ellis developed an eclectic design style that mixed architectural details in a particularly flamboyant way. By the time he was working on Cornwell, his own pet project at Portmeirion in North Wales – what he called his home for fallen buildings – was already well established. The then owner of Cornwell, Mrs Anthony Gillson, employed Williams-Ellis to modernise the village, but also to create the magnificent terraced gardens at the manor, along with building alterations. His influence may be clearly seen on the village hall (originally the school), with its bowed end and eccentric chimney stack-cum-bellcote.

The little Church of St Peter remained untouched at this time, though the handsome wooden candelabras are attributed to the style of Clough Williams-Ellis. It dates from Norman times, and it is believed that a village once surrounded the church, but disappeared during the plague years.

Churchill

In direct contrast to Cornwell, Churchill's attractions are up-front and open to view. The tower of All Saints' Church dominates the skyline for miles around, and if it looks familiar, that's because it's a scaled-down model of the tower of Magdalene College, Oxford. As the choristers of that famous establishment sing from their tower to greet the dawn on May Day, so local choristers gather at the top of All Saints' to do the same. The church was built in 1826 by James Langston, a mover and shaker in the village, and it is he who is affectionately remembered with the large and elaborate fountain next door.

Churchill boasts two famous sons. The first is Warren Hastings (1732–1818), a colourful figure who rose to become Governor-General of India, and lost his fortune in successfully defending himself against a charge of cruelty and corruption. The second is William Smith (1769–1839), who produced the first geological map of England.

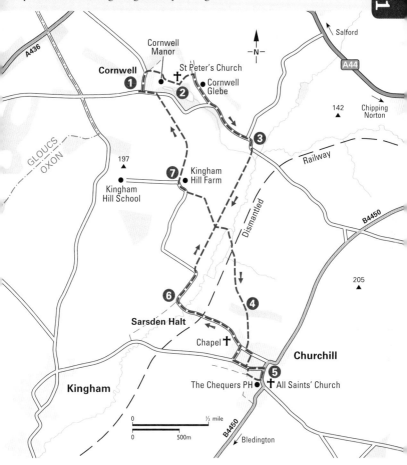

WALK 21 DIRECTIONS

❶ Turn left and walk down and up through Cornwell. Pass a farm, right, and turn right, signposted 'D'Arcy Dalton Way'. Where the track veers left, keep ahead, by a fingerpost. Walk down an orchard bearing left. Go through the hedge at the corner, and immediately through a metal gate on your left. Turn right and walk downhill. Go though a gate, right; follow the path towards St Peter's Church.

❷ Go through a gate into the churchyard. Pass the church, and leave via a squeeze gate. Walk straight ahead down the hill, cross the bridge at the bottom and go up to the gate. Turn right along the road, passing Cornwell Glebe. Bear left along the road and pass a left turning to Salford.

3 Turn right along a bridleway, signed 'Kingham'. Follow this for 0.5 mile (800m), go through a gate on the left and walk ahead down the field-edge. Cross a footbridge, go through a gate, and follow the path diagonally right. Cross another footbridge and bear right along the stream. Soon bear left and go through a gate. Cross the track and a footbridge opposite and bear diagonally right across the field corner. Cross a footbridge in a hedge and continue on through two fields.

WHAT TO LOOK OUT FOR

The hamlet of Sarsden Halt was once a stop on the railway line – hence the appearance and railway theme of some of its buildings. The line ran along the valley floor, linking Chipping Norton in the east with the main line at Kingham Station to the west. Its route is crossed twice in the course of the walk.

4 Cross a stile into the woods. Follow the path down, over a footbridge and right up the other side. Go through a gate and ahead towards Churchill. Cross a stile, then bear right beside a house. Cross a stile and turn left up the road. Pass a post-box and turn right along a path. At the next road turn left. At the top turn right.

5 Turn right again before you reach the church and follow the path round the back of The Chequers pub. Pass a barn and maintain your direction into a field. Soon turn right through a gate and walk down a grassy lane. At the road turn left; turn right at the next junction, then left at the end. Follow this road out of the village, passing the old chapel, now a heritage centre. Continue through Sarsden Halt.

WHERE TO EAT AND DRINK

Opposite the church, The Chequers in Churchill is an attractive old pub that has been lovingly renovated to provide an unexpected haven of fine dining. Sunday lunch is a highlight, but there are tasty sandwiches and a chiidren's menu if you want something lighter, and the beer is excellent, too. Dogs are welcome, but must stay outside during mealtimes

6 Follow the road right, then keep straight ahead along the green lane. After 0.3 mile (480m) go through a gate on your left and bear diagonally up the field. Walk up the hedge and turn right along the road.

7 Continue walking straight ahead through Kingham Hill Farm. Pass through a gate at the other side and carry on straight across two fields. Cross a stile, then a footbridge and stile and keep straight on. Pass an old gate and continue diagonally left up the field. Pass a marker post and continue through a gate bearing slightly right over the hill crest. Take the gate to the left of the main gate and turn left up the road to return to your car and the start of the walk.

WHILE YOU'RE THERE

Chipping Norton is the highest town in Oxfordshire, its wealth built on the wool trade. It centres on a large market square, with a little town hall dating from 1835 and some handsome Georgian frontages. There are lots of opportunities for shopping and eating out. The distinctive Bliss Valley Tweed Mill with its tall Tuscan-style chimney, on the north side of town, has been converted to flats.

Myths of the Rollright Stones

From Chipping Norton to an ancient site
associated with a charming legend.

DISTANCE *8 miles (12.9km)*   MINIMUM TIME *4hrs*

ASCENT/GRADIENT *295ft (90m)* ▲▲▲   LEVEL OF DIFFICULTY +++

PATHS *Field paths and tracks, country roads, 7 stiles*

LANDSCAPE *Rolling hills on the Oxfordshire/Warwickshire border*

SUGGESTED MAP *OS Explorer 191 Banbury, Bicester &*
Chipping Norton

START / FINISH *Grid reference: SP 313271*

DOG FRIENDLINESS *Under control or on lead across farmland, one lengthy*
stretch of country road and busy streets in Chipping Norton

PARKING *Free car park off A44, in centre of Chipping Norton*

PUBLIC TOILETS *At car park*

Commanding a splendid position overlooking the hills and valleys of the north-east Cotswolds, the Rollright Stones comprise the Whispering Knights, the King's Men and the King Stone. These intriguing stones are steeped in myth and legend.

Mystical Theories

It seems a king was leading his army in this quiet corner of Oxfordshire while five of his knights stood together conspiring against him. The king met a witch near by who told him he would be King of England if he could see the settlement of Long Compton in seven long strides. As he approached the top of the ridge a mound of earth suddenly rose up before him, preventing him from seeing the village and so the king, his soldiers and his knights were all turned to stone.

In reality the Rollright Stones form a group of prehistoric megalithic monuments created from large natural boulders found within about 600yds (549m) of the site. The stones are naturally pitted, giving them astonishing and highly unusual shapes. The five Whispering Knights are the remains of a Portal Dolmen burial chamber, probably from 3800–3000 BC, long before the stone circle. It would have been imposing in its day and it is the easternmost burial chamber of this kind in Britain. The King Stone stands apart from the others The 8ft (2.4m) tall single standing stone was almost certainly erected to mark the site of a Bronze Age cemetery which was in use around 1800–1500 BC.

Finally, you come to the King's Men Stone Circle – a ceremonial monument thought to have been built around 2500–2000 BC. There are over 70 stones here. Originally there were about 105 stones forming a continuous wall except for one narrow entrance. The King's Men Stones are arranged in an unditched circle about 100ft (30m) across and ranging in size from just a few inches to 7ft (2m). Here and there the stones are so close they almost touch.

CHIPPING NORTON

It is not clear what the stone circle was used for but it may well have had some significance in religious and secular ceremonies. Most mysterious of all is why this particular site was chosen. Visitors to the Rollright Stones have questioned their origin but they remain a mystery.

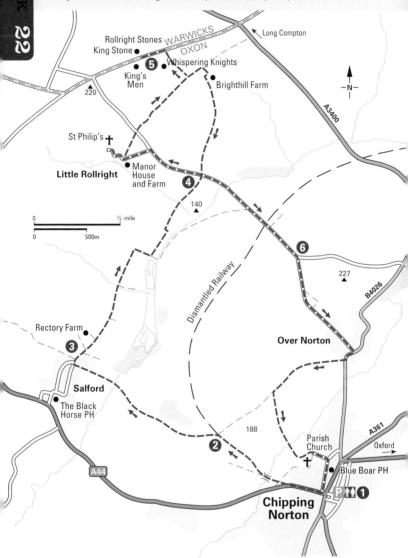

WALK 22 DIRECTIONS

1 Follow the A44, New Street, downhill. Pass Penhurst School, then veer right through a kissing gate. Skirt the left-hand edge of the recreation ground and aim for a gate. Descend to a bridge and,

when the path forks, keep right. Go up the slope to a kissing gate. Cross a drive and continue to the next tarmac drive. Keep ahead to a stile and along the right-hand edge of a field. Make for gate and drop down to some double gates on the right.

WHERE TO EAT AND DRINK

Chipping Norton offers a variety of pubs, hotels and tea rooms. Try the rambling old Blue Boar with its views of the Market Place and the town's many historic buildings. Here you'll find a good choice of dishes, including Gloucestershire sausages and baked rabbit. The Black Horse at Salford offers the chance to stop off for refreshment during the walk.

❷ Go through. Turn sharp left and walk towards Salford, keeping the hedge on the left. Continue into the village and soon turn right by some grass and a sign, 'Trout Lakes – Rectory Farm'.

❸ Follow the track to a right-hand bend. Go straight ahead here, following the field edge. Make for a gate ahead and turn right in the next field. About 100yds (91m) before the field corner, turn left and follow the path across to an opening in the boundary. Veer left, then immediately right to skirt the field. Cross a little stream and maintain your direction in the next field to reach the road.

WHILE YOU'RE THERE

Have a look at Chipping Norton, or 'Chippy' as the locals call it. One of the gateways to the Cotswolds, the town prospered as a result of the wool trade. The church, though not prominently placed in the town, is impressive.

❹ Turn left, then left again for Little Rollright. After visiting the church, retrace your steps to the D'Arcy Dalton Way on the left. Follow the path up the field slope to the road. Cross over and continue on the way between fields. Head for some trees and approach a stile. Don't

cross it; instead, turn left and skirt the field, passing close to the Whispering Knights.

❺ On reaching the road, turn left and visit the site of the Rollright Stones. Return to the Whispering Knights, head down the field to the stile and cross it to an immediate second stile. Walk ahead along a grassy path and turn right at the next stile towards Brighthill Farm. Pass alongside the buildings to a stile, head diagonally right down the field to a double stile, keep the boundary on your right and head for a galvanised gate in the bottom right corner of the field. Make for the bottom right corner of the next field, go through a gate and skirt the field, turning left at the road.

WHAT TO LOOK OUT FOR

The manor house at Little Rollright was once important. It was the home of William Blower who gave St Philip's Church its pinnacled tower in 1617. The church, which dates mostly from the 15th century, has two 17th-century monuments to the local Dixon and Blower families.

❻ Keep right at the next fork and head towards the village of Over Norton. Walk through the village to the T-junction. Turn right and when the road swings to the left by Cleeves Corner, join a track signposted 'Salford'. When the hedges on the left give way, look for a waymark on the left. Follow the path down the slope, make for two kissing gates and then follow the path alongside a stone wall to reach the parish church. Join Church Lane and follow it as far as the T-junction. Turn right and return to the town centre.

Regenerating Bourton-on-the-Water

*On the wilder side of Bourton-on-the-Water
to see its natural regeneration.*

WALK 23

DISTANCE 5 miles (8km)   **MINIMUM TIME** 2hrs 30min

ASCENT/GRADIENT 230ft (70m) ▲▲▲   **LEVEL OF DIFFICULTY** ✚✚✚

PATHS Track and field, can be muddy and wet in places, 20 stiles

LANDSCAPE Sweeping valley views, lakes, streams, hills and village

SUGGESTED MAP OS Explorer OL45 The Cotswolds

START / FINISH Grid reference: SP 169208

DOG FRIENDLINESS Some stiles may be awkward for dogs; occasional livestock

PARKING Pay-and-display car park on Station Road

PUBLIC TOILETS At car park

Despite Bourton-on-the-Water's popularity the throng is easily left behind by walking briefly eastwards to a chain of redundant gravel pits. In the 1970s these were landscaped and filled with water and fish. As is the way of these things, for some time the resulting lakes looked every inch the artificial creations they were, but now they have bedded into their surroundings and seem to be an integral part of the landscape.

Migrating Birds

The fish and water have acted as magnets for a range of wetland birds, whose populations rise and fall with the seasons. During the spring and summer you should look out for the little grebe and the splendidly adorned great crested grebe, as well as the more familiar moorhens and coots, and mallard and tufted ducks. Wagtails will strut about the water's edge, swans and geese prowl across the water and kingfishers, if you are lucky, streak from bush to reed. Come the autumn, the number of birds will have increased significantly. Above all there will be vast numbers of ducks – pintail, shoveler, widgeon and pochard among them – as well as occasional visitors like cormorants. Either around the lakes or by the rivers you may also spy dippers and, in the hedgerows, members of the finch family.

Immigrant Birds

Should you get drawn into the village – as you surely will – keep listening for birdsong and you will hear some improbable 'visitors'. Bourton-on-the-Water has a large bird sanctuary which houses, among many other birds, one of the largest collections of penguins in the world. The reason for the presence of so many penguins in the Cotswolds is that the sanctuary's founder was also the owner of two small islands in the Falklands.

Long History

Penguins aside, Bourton-on-the-Water has a long history. The edge of the village is bounded by the Roman Fosse Way and many of its buildings are a pleasing mix of medieval, Georgian and Victorian. Although the village can become very crowded during the summer months, with the river banks at its centre like green beaches, strewn with people picnicking and paddling, it can still be charming. Arrive early enough in the morning, or hang around in the evening until the daytrippers have gone and you will find the series of bridges spanning the Windrush (one from 1756) and the narrow streets beyond them highly picturesque. They retain the warm honeyed light that attracts people to the Cotswolds. You'll see far fewer visitors in little Clapton-on-the-Hill, which overlooks Bourton. Make the brief detour just before Point ❺ to see its handsome green and tiny church.

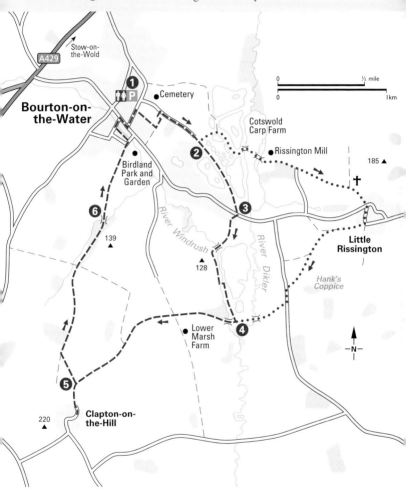

WALK 23 DIRECTIONS

❶ Opposite the entrance to the main pay-and-display car park in Bourton-on-the-Water locate a public footpath to the right of the coach depot and continue to a junction opposite the village

cemetery. Bear right to follow a lane all the way to its end. There are two gates in front of you. Take the one on the right-hand side, to join a grassy track.

❷ Follow the track between lakes to where it curves right. Leave the

WHERE TO EAT AND DRINK

There are no pubs in Clapton. Bourton-on-the-Water has pubs, teashops and restaurants, catering to most tastes. Try the Kingsbridge Inn by the River Windrush, or the Mousetrap on Lansdown for reliable pub food. The Old Manse, near the river, serves a good lunch and dinner.

track to go left and over a bridge and stile into a field. Go across the field, curving right, to come to a kissing gate at a road.

❸ Cross the road, turn right and immediately left on to a track. After 100yds (91m) go left through a kissing gate into a field and continue parallel to the track. Through a kissing gate, return to the track, with a lake to your left. Just before a gate turn right over a bridge and left through a kissing gate on to a path alongside the River Windrush. Continue until the path comes to a stile at a field. Turn left, go through another kissing gate and go left over a bridge before turning right beside another lake.

WHILE YOU'RE THERE

Bourton-on-the-Water has many and diverse attractions. The pick of these are probably Birdland Park and Garden (See Background to the Walk) with their penguins, and the Cotswold Motor Museum, which has lots of pre-1950s cars as well as a few novelty items to thrill children.

❹ Where this second, smaller lake ends bear right to a stile, followed by a bridge and another bridge and a stile at a field. Keep to the right side of fields until you come to a track after one kissing gate. At a house continue straight on leaving the track and continue to a stile. In the next field, after 25yds (23m), turn left over a stile and then sharp right. Continue to a stile and then go half left across a field to a stile. Continue on the same line across the next field to a kissing gate, footbridge and gate. Cross this and follow the right margin of a field, to climb slowly to a junction of tracks. Turn left to visit the village of Clapton-on-the-Hill, or turn right to continue.

❺ Follow a track to a field. Go forward then half right to a stile and descend to pass right of woodland. Past this continue alongside a hedge on your left to a stile, followed by two stiles together at a field. Go half left to a stile and after another stile a stream appears to the left. Keep on this side of the stream and pass through a copse and another stile. The path then turns left over a footbridge with a stile at each end.

❻ Cross the bridge and then go half right across a field to a bridge. Walk along a grassy track between conifers towards house. Go through one more gate and follow a path between fences to a road in Bourton. Walk ahead to the river and turn left, then right past a riverside café, then right again, and left to return to the start.

EXTENDING THE WALK

You can extend this walk to include the pretty village of Little Rissington. As you leave Bourton on the lane after the cemetery, at Point ❷, follow a path to the left, past lakes and meadows to Rissington Mill. Field paths take you into the village and you can meet up with the main route again across the bridge near Point ❹.

Right: Bourton-on-the-Water

Painswick's Traditions

From the Queen of the Cotswolds through the Washpool Valley.

DISTANCE 7.5 miles (12.1km)   **MINIMUM TIME** 3hrs 30min

ASCENT/GRADIENT 705ft (215m) ▲▲▲   **LEVEL OF DIFFICULTY** +++

PATHS Fields, tracks, golf course and a green lane, 20 stiles

LANDSCAPE Hills, valleys, villages, isolated farmhouses, extensive views

SUGGESTED MAP OS Explorer 179 Gloucester, Cheltenham & Stroud

START / FINISH Grid reference: SO 865095

DOG FRIENDLINESS Off lead along lengthy stretches, many stiles

PARKING Car park (small fee) near library, just off main road, Painswick

PUBLIC TOILETS At car park

Local traditions continue to thrive in Painswick, the 'Queen of the Cotswolds'. These are centred around its well-known churchyard, where the Victorian poet Sydney Dobell is buried. The churchyard is famously filled, not only with the 'table' tombs of 18th-century clothiers, but also with 99 beautifully manicured yew trees, planted in 1792. The legend goes that only 99 will ever grow at any one time, as Old Nick will always kill off the hundredth. Should you be minded to do so, try to count them. You will almost certainly be thwarted, as many of them have grown together, creating arches and hedges.

This old tale has become confused with an ancient ceremony that still takes place here on the Sunday nearest to the Feast of the Nativity of St Mary, in mid-September. This is the 'clipping' ceremony, which has nothing to do with cutting bushes or flowers. It derives from the old Saxon word, 'clyping', which means 'embrace' and is used in conjunction with the church. Traditionally, the children of the village gather together on the Sunday afternoon and join hands to form a circle around the church or churchyard, and advance and retreat to and from the church, singing the *Clipping Hymn*. Perhaps this ceremony is the distant descendant of an a pagan ceremony involving a ritual dance around an altar bearing a sacrificed animal. The children wear flowers in their hair and are rewarded with a coin and a bun for their efforts. There was, and maybe still is, a special cake baked for the day, known as 'puppy dog pie', in which a small china dog was inserted. Was this a reminder of the ancient ritual sacrifice? There are yew trees in other gardens in the village, many older than those in the churchyard, and one of which is said to have been planted by Elizabeth I.

The other famous tradition that continues to be observed in the area takes place further along the escarpment, at Cooper's Hill. Here, on Spring Bank Holiday Monday, the cheese-rolling races take place. From a spot marked by a maypole, competitors hurtle down an absurdly steep slope in pursuit of wooden discs representing Gloucester cheeses. The winner, or survivor, is presented with a real cheese; but the injury rate is high and there has been a lot of controversy about whether the event should continue.

Left: St Mary's Church, Painswick

PAINSWICK

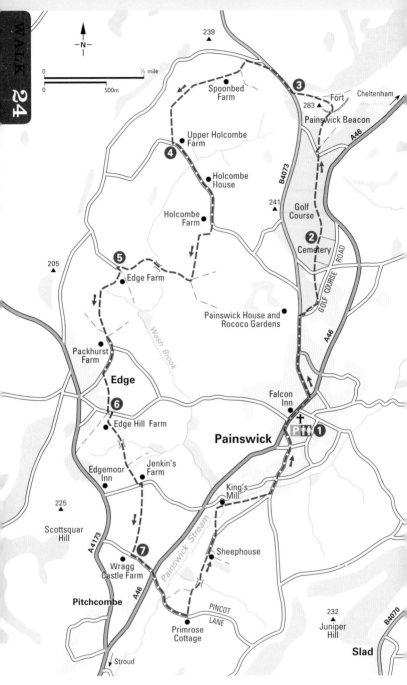

WALK 24 DIRECTIONS

❶ Turn right out of the car park and right along the main street.

Turn left along Gloucester Street, join another road and continue uphill, then go right on to Golf Course Road. Bear left on to a track, joining the Cotswold Way, through the ramblers' car park, turn left into a lane and then, after 50 paces go left into woodland and then across a fairway (look out for flying golf balls).

2 Keep to the left of a cemetery, then cross another fairway to a woodland path. Continue to a road. After 50 paces turn right, leaving the track after 60 paces. Walk along the left edge of the golf course to the top of a promontory, passing to the right of a trig point. Descend the other side and turn left down a path. At a track go left to a road, aiming for the gap in the trees visible from the trig point.

3 Turn right and descend to a bus stop by the 50mph sign. Here cross to a path diverging from the road amid trees. Beyond a gate turn left down a track to Spoonbed Farm, and descend bearing right at a track junction. Pass the farm to a gate, then take a path to a field. In a second field keep left of an ash tree to reach a stile. Through a new copse and after another stile cross a field to the right of an electricity pole and farm buildings. Keep right of Upper Holcombe Farm to a stile.

4 Turn left on to a lane rising for 0.5 mile (800m) to Holcombe Farm. Here continue straight on along a track, passing some gates at a bend on the left. Continue and at a stile go left into the next field. Cross another stile and bear right to another stile. Over this

turn right into a green lane which leads to a footbridge with a stile at each end. Bear right alongside the stream and soon bear left uphill through trees to a stile. Over this follow the left-hand field margin curving uphill to a stile.

5 Turn left along a track towards Edge Farm and then fork right at farm buildings to a gate. Over a stone stile cross two fields to another gate soon arriving at a road. Bear right at a Y-junction. Opposite a house turn left over a stile, bear half right to another stile and on to a path between a hedge and a fence to enter Edge.

6 Turn left, then sharp right at the post-box and go past the village hall. Before the farmhouse turn left over a stile, then another and descend along the field margin to a footbridge. Over this ascend a field to a stile in the opposite hedge, then head for a gate at a track, to the right of a farm. Go through this and through another gate opposite and then along field edge to a kissing gate on to a lane. Turn left and, after 30 paces, turn right via a gate on to a track. The track becomes a path to a stile. Cross fields on the same line, then over stile and quarter left to a field gate and then another, passing right by a house to a road.

7 Turn left, descend to cross the A46 and walk along Pincot Lane. At Primrose Cottage turn left over a stile and then cross to another. Descend to cross a footbridge, climb and cross the field to a gate, left of Sheephouse. Walk along the drive and where it forks go left down to King's Mill. Bear right through a gate and over the weir, then a stile, and walk alongside the stream to arrive at a lane, via two more stiles. Turn left to return to Painswick.

The Medieval Looters of Brimpsfield

A walk through a vanished castle and secluded valleys, taking in charming Syde and tiny Caudle Green.

DISTANCE *4 miles (6.4km)* MINIMUM TIME *2hrs*

ASCENT/GRADIENT *180ft (55m)* ▲▲▲ LEVEL OF DIFFICULTY ✦✦✦

PATHS *Fields, tracks and pavement, 18 stiles*

LANDSCAPE *Woodland, steep, narrow valleys and villages*

SUGGESTED MAP *OS Explorer 179 Gloucester, Cheltenham & Stroud*

START / FINISH *Grid reference: SO 938127*

DOG FRIENDLINESS *Some good, long stretches free of livestock*

PARKING *Brimpsfield Village Hall car park (in north-west of village)*

PUBLIC TOILETS *None en route*

There is something poignant about a vanished castle. The manor of Brimpsfield was given by William the Conqueror to the Giffard family. In early Norman French a 'gifard' was a person with fat cheeks and a double chin. The Giffards built two castles, the first of wood on another site, and its successor of stone, near Brimpsfield church. In 1322 John Giffard fell foul of King Edward II, following a rebellion that was quelled at the Battle of Boroughbridge in Yorkshire – Giffard was hanged at Gloucester.

Plundering Populace

Consequently the family castle was 'slighted', that is to say, put beyond military use. In such circumstances local people were never slow to remove what was left for their own, non-military use. Now almost nothing remains of the castle apart from the empty meadow just before the church and some earthworks to its right. Some of the castle masonry found its way into the fabric of the church. On the stone shed to the left of the church there are details that appear to be medieval and which perhaps originally decorated the castle. The other possibility is that they formed part of a 12th-century priory, long since disappeared, that belonged to the abbey of Fontenay in Burgundy. Brimpsfield church, rather lonely without its castle, distinguishes itself on two counts. Several medieval tombstones, thought to commemorate members of the Giffard family, have been brought inside for their protection.

Mysterious Masonry

The other, highly unusual feature, is the huge base of the tower, which separates the nave from the chancel. It is not clear how this came about, but it is surmised that the east wall would originally have contained an arch over which a bell turret was built in the 13th century, requiring the addition of more masonry. When the turret was replaced by a 15th-century tower still more masonry was needed to keep it upright.

Syde overlooks the Frome Valley and perched on the valley slope, the early Norman church has a saddleback tower and a rustic, 15th-century roof. It's worth peering inside to search out the 15th-century octagonal font and the small round window featuring St James, dating from the same period. The box pews are from the 17th century. Don't miss the tithe barn just to the south of the church. Caudle Green is a typical example of a hamlet that has grown up around a single farm and expanded only very slightly over the centuries. It is dominated by an elegant 18th-century farmhouse overlooking the village green.

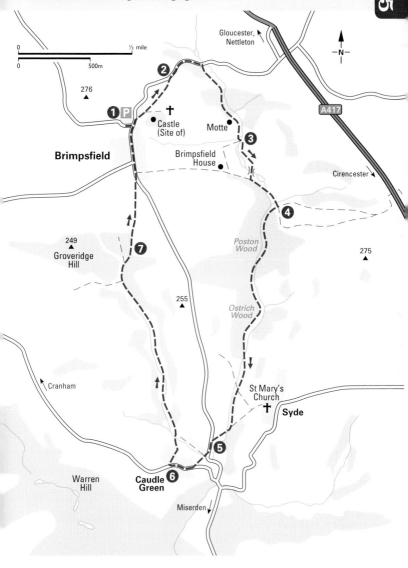

WALK 25 DIRECTIONS

❶ From the Brimpsfield Village Hall car park head back into the village. By the bus stop, cross to a gate, signed 'To Church'. Before you reach the church bear left to a stile. In the next field go half right to a corner and then go over a stile on to a road.

2 Turn right and follow the road down to just before a cottage near the bottom. Turn right on to a drive. After 35 paces drop down to the left on to a parallel path which will bring you back on to the drive. Next, just before a cottage, turn left and go down into woodland to follow a path (the stream on your left). Follow this for 550yds (503m), ignoring a bridge on your left, to cross two stiles and emerge on to a track.

WHILE YOU'RE THERE

In nearby Miserden the Elizabethan mansion, Misarden Park, is set in pretty gardens; they are open on certain days throughout the summer months. Sir Edward Lutyens designed the war memorial here. Further west is Whiteway, where a group of libertarians from Essex established a proto-anarchist community, based on the ideas of Leo Tolstoy, in 1898.

3 Turn left and follow the track as it rises to the right. After 100yds (91m), where the track bears left, go forward over a stile into a field with Brimpsfield House to your right. Go half right to another stile, pass a gate on your right and cross another stile at the next corner amid scrub. Follow the path to cross a bridge and bear left up to a track. Follow this for 250yds (229m), until you come to a crossways, just past two pollarded willows.

4 Turn right through a gate to follow a footpath along the bottom of a wooded valley. After 0.75 mile (1.2km) the track will become grassy. Where houses appear above you to the left you can go left up the slope to visit the church at Syde. Otherwise remain on the valley floor and continue until you come to a gate. Go

WHERE TO EAT AND DRINK

There is nowhere on the route where refreshment is available, unless you divert to the Golden Hart at Nettleton Bottom. Otherwise you can seek out the Carpenter's Arms in Miserden to the south, or the Black Horse in Cranham to the west.

through it, then over a stile to pass to the left of a cottage. Follow a drive up to a road.

5 Turn left and follow the road until it turns sharp left. At this point turn right over a stile into a field and walk up a steep bank and over a stone stile to arrive on a road in Caudle Green.

6 Turn right. At the green, just before a large Georgian house ahead of you, and follow a winding path in woodland down to the valley bottom. Over a stile, turn left, go through a bridle gate, and follow the path along the valley bottom on the same line for 0.75 mile (1.2km) until you come to a stile at a field.

7 Walk along edge of a wood, then up valley to a stile. Over this continue alongside a hedge until you come to a stile at a road. Turn left to re-enter Brimpsfield village, continuing past a telephone box, go left at the war memorial and back to the Village Hall.

WHAT TO LOOK OUT FOR

The little stream encountered at certain points during the walk is the infant River Frome, which, in its later, stronger stages to the south, runs through the Stroud Valley. As you ascend the valley slope into Syde look out for the old sheep dip just below the village.

Musing on the Past at Northleach

*A modest Cotswold market town is home to
a pair of diverse museums.*

DISTANCE *4 miles (6.4km)*   MINIMUM TIME *1hr 45min*

ASCENT/GRADIENT *165ft (50m)* ▲▲▲   LEVEL OF DIFFICULTY +++

PATHS *Fields, tracks and pavement, muddy after rain, 3 stiles*

LANDSCAPE *Valley track, wolds and villages*

SUGGESTED MAP *OS Explorer OL45 The Cotswolds*

START / FINISH *Grid reference: SP 113145*

DOG FRIENDLINESS *Some clear stretches without livestock, few stiles*

PARKING *Northleach market place*

PUBLIC TOILETS *In market place*

For a small market town to have one museum is unusual – to have two, as Northleach does, is remarkable. One, the Cotswold Countryside Collection, is closely associated with its surroundings; the other, Keith Harding's World of Mechanical Music, is one of those eccentricities that has, by happenstance, ended up here in Northleach.

Mechanical Music Museum

The World of Mechanical Music is in the High Street at Oak House, a former wool house, pub and school. There are daily demonstrations of all manner of mechanical musical instruments, as well as musical boxes, clocks and automata. Some of the instruments, early examples of 'canned' music, date back more than 200 years. The presentation is simultaneously erudite and light-hearted. (You may also listen to early, live recordings of concerts given by some of the great composers including Gershwin and Grieg.) This is something more than a museum – both serious historical research and highly accomplished repairs are carried out here.

House of Correction

To the west of the town centre, at a corner of a Fosse Way crossroads, lies the Cotswold Countryside Collection. It is housed in an 18th-century prison, or 'house of correction', built by a prison reformer and wealthy philanthropist, Sir Onesiphorous Paul. He was a descendant of a family of successful clothiers from Woodchester, near Stroud, who were also responsible for the construction of, what is now, the Prince of Wales's house at Highgrove. Paul's intentions were surely good, but conditions in the prison were still harsh and the treadmill was still considered effective as the unrelenting instrument of slow punishment. As well as a restored 18th-century cell block, you'll find the museum houses an interesting collection of agricultural implements and machinery, and displays plenty of fascinating photographs showing what rural life in the Cotswolds was once like. It is also the offices of the Chilterns Conservation Board.

Then and Now

Northleach itself, like Cirencester and Chipping Campden, was one of the key medieval wool trading centres of the Cotswolds. Though once on a crossroads of the A40 and the Fosse Way, neither now passes through the town, the completion of the A40 bypass in the mid-1980s leaving the town centre a quiet and very attractive place to visit.

The main street is lined with houses, some half-timbered, dating from the 16th to 19th centuries. Many of these retain their ancient 'burgage' rear plots that would have served as market gardens. Above the market square is a tiny maze of narrow lanes, overlooked by the Church of St Peter and St Paul, the town's impressive 15th-century Perpendicular 'wool church'.

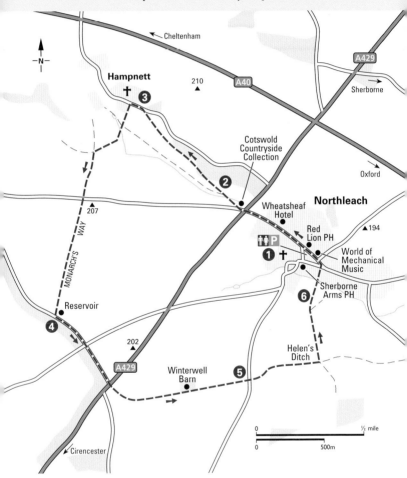

WALK 26 DIRECTIONS

❶ From Northleach market place, with the church behind you, turn left and walk along the main street to the traffic lights at the A429. Cross with care, keep left of the Cotswold Countryside Collection and, immediately after passing the museum, turn right through a gate into a field. Go half right to cross a stream by a field corner and into the next field.

② Aiming for a church tower go half right up the field to a gate. Pass through this into the next field and, keeping fairly close to the field's right-hand margin, head for a kissing gate on the far side. Pass into the next field and follow a path across it in the general direction of Hampnett church. This will bring you to a kissing gate at a road.

③ Turn left and almost immediately come to a concrete track on your left. To visit the church walk ahead and then return to this track. Otherwise, turn left down the track and follow it as it descends to pass farm buildings. Where the track begins to bear right, turn left to climb a track towards a gate. Go through it and continue to follow the track, eventually striking a road. Cross this to walk along another track all the way to another road by a reservoir.

④ At this road turn left and walk until you reach the A429. Cross with great care to a gate and then

walk along a grassy track until you come to a farmyard. Walk through the yard and out the other side along a track to another road.

⑤ Cross to a track and follow this for 500yds (457m). Turn left through a gap in a hedge to enter a field and follow the left margin with a stone wall to your left. Northleach will soon come into view. Where the field comes to an end, go through a kissing gate and descend alongside a fence to a kissing gate beside a playground.

⑥ Go through and skirt tennis courts to cross a stream. Walk the length of an alley and, at the top, turn left to return to the starting point.

Sherborne and the Sherborne Estate

A walk from a picturesque village through the woods and parkland of an 18th-century estate once owned by wealthy Winchcombe Abbey.

DISTANCE 2.5 miles (4km) **MINIMUM TIME** 1hr 15min

ASCENT/GRADIENT 188ft (57m) ▲▲▲ **LEVEL OF DIFFICULTY** ✦✦✦

PATHS Fields, track and pavement

LANDSCAPE Village and landscaped estate

SUGGESTED MAP OS Explorer OL45 The Cotswolds

START / FINISH Grid reference: SP 175144

DOG FRIENDLINESS No stiles and some clear stretches without livestock

PARKING Village street

PUBLIC TOILETS None en route

Sherborne was always an estate village, originally belonging to Winchcombe Abbey. Huge flocks of sheep were gathered here for shearing, with much of the wool exported to Flanders and Italy. In the 14th century the tenants of the Abbot of Winchcombe had to work for a fortnight washing and shearing the abbey's sheep.

Abbey Habits

A century later Sherborne, because of the plentiful water supply provided by the river, essential for washing the wool, and because it was the largest of the abbey's manorial possessions, had become the principal shearing station for all the abbey's flocks. In 1485 drovers brought in 2,900 sheep from the surrounding 'holdings', or villages. Quarters were provided for all the shearers while the Abbot of Winchcombe rode up to supervise and inspect the weighing of the fleeces in a room set aside for the purpose.
He bought as much of the tenants' wool as he required and then sold it on. The abbot of course wanted to make sure that he made as much money as possible; and indeed in 1341 local tenants were fined by their abbot for attempting to set up a fulling mill in competition with his own.

Sherborne Estate

After the Dissolution, the estate was purchased by the Dutton family, who built themselves a fine house with the help of the eminent local quarryman, Valentine Strong. In the 19th century the house, said to be haunted by the hunchback and gambler known as 'Crump' Dutton, was rebuilt using estate stone but eventually it became a boarding school and has now been converted into luxury flats. Today the estate, and much of the village, belongs to the National Trust. The village of Sherborne has some very pretty cottages, one of which, in the eastern part, has somehow acquired a Norman arch, which originally graced a 12th-century chapel that apparently stood in the grounds of one of the nearby farms. From the road near the church are sweeping rustic views across Sherborne Brook and its water-meadows, where once the medieval flocks of sheep would have grazed.

SHERBORNE

Lodge Park

South of Sherborne, near the village of Aldsworth, is Lodge Park, originally part of the Sherborne Estate. This was created in 1634 by 'Crump' Dutton and is a unique survival of a deer course, park and grandstand, which has been painstakingly reconstructed using archaeological evidence.

Sherborne was also the birthplace of an eminent scientist. James Bradley, born here in 1693, was appointed the third Astronomer Royal in 1742, and is remembered as the first person to calculate the speed of light in 1729. He also established the time line at Greenwich.

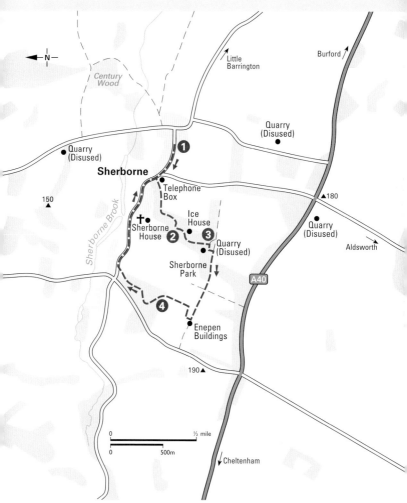

WALK 27 DIRECTIONS

❶ From the main part of the village, east of the church, walk back towards Sherborne House. Continue to a road on the left beside the war memorial. Enter the Sherborne Estate through a doorway beside the telephone box and follow the main path. The route is waymarked by signs with a white bootprint on a blue arrow. The house will appear to the right. The path bears sharp left and

97

WHERE TO EAT AND DRINK

There is nowhere to eat or drink on the route itself, although you'll find the small post office and store in Sherborne is a useful place to stock up on snacks. The nearest pub is The Fox Inn, just outside Little Barrington, about 2.5 miles (4km) away to the east in the Windrush Valley. It has a lovely riverside location, a good range of locally brewed real ales and an extensive menu.

after 150yds (137m) turns right at a bench. After a further 150yds (137m) turn left on to another gently ascending path.

2 Stay left of a tree surrounded by a metal seat on a mound and take a path on the far side to head for a gate. Go through the smaller, right-hand one of two gates, pass the old Ice House and head for another gate, following waymarks.

3 Follow the main path through the trees. Join another path and, at a gate, go through on to a farm track and turn right. Follow this, passing a cricket pitch on

the left, to a gate at a farmyard. Go through this and turn right straight away to pass through another gateway. Immediately past a gate on the right, turn right into a field to follow the right-hand margin. Follow this as it bears left at the corner and descend to the bottom corner where the path will take you into conifer woodland. Follow this wide path down until you come to a fork.

4 Stay left and keep to the path as it skirts the woods, bearing right to flatten out at the bottom. Stay on it all the way to an opening in a wall. Emerge at a road and turn right. Follow the pavement through the village, passing the church on the right, and return to your starting point.

WHAT TO LOOK OUT FOR

Sherborne Park is a typical example of 18th-century estate design, where the intention has been to bring order to unruly nature without undermining its exuberance. The estate is now owned and managed by the National Trust. In the church, look out for the sculpture to the Dutton family by Flemish-born John Michael Rysbrack (1694–1770), a respected sculptor and best known for his monument to Sir Isaac Newton in Westminster Abbey. There is also a memorial in the village church to the locally born Astronomer Royal, James Bradley.

WHILE YOU'RE THERE

The walk can easily and briefly be extended by walking a little way east of Sherborne to a point east of Century Wood, where the old water-meadows have been restored to become a haven for wildlife once again.

Right: Windrush River from The Fox Inn near Little Barrington

The Stone Secrets of the Windrush Valley

*An insight into the character of Cotswold stone,
which makes up the building blocks of the region's beauty.*

DISTANCE *6 miles (9.7km)* **MINIMUM TIME** *2hrs 30min*

ASCENT/GRADIENT *120ft (37m)* ▲▲▲ **LEVEL OF DIFFICULTY** ✦✦✦

PATHS *Fields, tracks and pavement, 14 stiles*

LANDSCAPE *Streams, fields, open country and villages*

SUGGESTED MAP *OS Explorer OL45 The Cotswolds*

START / FINISH *Grid reference: SP 192131*

DOG FRIENDLINESS *Some care required but can probably be off lead for
long stretches without livestock*

PARKING *Windrush village*

PUBLIC TOILETS *None en route*

The Cotswolds, characterised by villages of gilded stone, lie mainly in Gloucestershire. Stone is everywhere here – walk across any field and shards of oolitic limestone lie about the surface like bits of fossilised litter. This limestone, for long an obstacle to arable farming, is a perfect building material. In the past almost every village was served by its own quarry, a few of which are still worked today.

Golden Hue

Limestone is a sedimentary rock, made largely of material derived from living organisms that thrived in the sea that once covered this part of Britain. The rock is therefore easily extracted and easily worked; some of it will actually yield to a handsaw. Of course this is something of a generalisation as, even in a small area, the quality of limestone varies considerably in colour and in texture, suiting certain uses more than others. But it is for its golden hue, due to the presence of iron oxide, that it is most famous.

Slated

The composition of the stone dictates the use to which it will be put. Some limestone, with a high proportion of grit, is best suited to wall building or to hut building. Some outcrops are in very thin layers and are known as 'presents' because they provide almost ready-made material for roof-slates. When the stone needs a little help it is left out in the winter so that frost freezes the moisture trapped between layers, forcing them apart. The stone can then be shaped into slates and hung on a wooden roof trellis by means of a simple nail. The smallest slates are placed at the top of the roof, the largest at the bottom. Because of their porous nature, they have to overlap and the roof is built at a steep pitch, so that the rain runs off quickly.

Construction Types

There are four basic types of traditional stone construction to be seen in the Cotswolds – dry-stone, mortared rubble, dressed stone and ashlar.

Left: Doorway of the Norman church of St Peter's, Windrush

WINDRUSH

Dry-stone, without any mortar, is used in the many boundary walls you'll see as you walk around the region. Mortared rubble, on the other hand, depends on the use of lime pointing in order to stay upright. You'll see its use in many of the simpler buildings or as a cheaper backing to buildings faced with better stone. Dressed stone refers to the craft of chopping and axing stone to give it a more polished and tighter finish. This is used in higher order buildings and houses.

Ashlar is the finest technique, where the best stone is expertly sawn and shaped into perfectly aligned blocks that act either as a facing on rubble, or which, more rarely, make up the entire wall. Ashlar was used in the region's finer houses and, occasionally, in barns. The quality of Cotswold stone has long been recognised and the quarries here, to the west of Burford, provided building material for London's St Paul's Cathedral and several Oxford colleges.

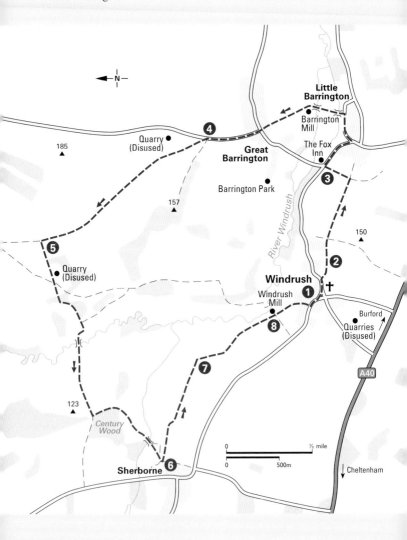

WALK 28 DIRECTIONS

1 Walk out of the village, keeping to the left of the church and, after about 100yds (91m), go right, opposite No 27, through a kissing gate into a field. Go across this field to the other side, keeping to the left.

2 Go through the right-hand gate and continue across a series of stiles until you emerge in a large field at a wide grass strip (careful here, as it is used for 'galloping' horses) with the houses of Little Barrington opposite. Cross two thirds of the field, then turn left and head for the hedge at the bottom to the right of the cricket field.

3 Go through a gap to the road. Ahead is The Fox Inn. Turn right, the pub car park on your left, enter Little Barrington and turn left along a 'No Through Road'. Pass Sundial Cottage on your left, the lane soon narrowing to a path. Where the path becomes a lane again, go left across a bridge, then another and pass to the right of Barrington Mill. Continue, eventually emerging in Great Barrington at a war memorial cross. Take the road in front of you, 'Little Rissington and Bourton-on-the-Water'.

4 Where the stone park wall to Barrington Park on your left ends, go left on to a track and immediately right through a gate. Stay on this track for a little over 1 mile (1.6km) until, after climbing out of a dry valley, you come to a junction of tracks with large hedges before you.

5 Turn sharp left and follow this track to the valley bottom and, where it turns hard left, go straight on and enter scrubby

woodland. Cross the bridge over the River Windrush and follow a grassy track for two fields until, just before Century Wood, you turn left over a bridge with a stile at each end into a field. Follow the margin of the woods. Cross another bridge and a stile into a field and turn half right to the far corner. Through a gate, cross a footbridge and, after 50 paces, go through another gate and go half left to another stile.

6 Take the track before you and then turn left over another stile. Cross this field parallel to the left-hand wall to go through a gate and walk along the right-hand margin of the next three fields.

7 Continue to reach a stile at a corner. Go over into the next field and cross it on a right diagonal, walking in the general direction of a distant village. On the far side go through a gap into another field, with a stone wall on your right. Continue over a stone stile for several fields and pass by a stone barn to your right, at which point the River Windrush will appear to your left. Finally, pass a tin barn to your left-hand side, just as you arrive at a gate by a lane.

8 Opposite, go up to a stile. Follow the perimeter of the next field as it goes right, ignoring a footpath into a field at the corner. Go beside a stone wall, over a stone stile on to a narrow track which leads into Windrush village.

Wanderings at Wychwood

A gentle walk through rolling Oxfordshire farmland and a corner of an ancient forest.

DISTANCE *5.75 miles (9.2km)* MINIMUM TIME *3hrs*

ASCENT/GRADIENT *574ft (175m)* ▲▲▲ LEVEL OF DIFFICULTY +++

PATHS *Field paths, quiet roads, woodland tracks, no stiles*

LANDSCAPE *Gently rolling hills of arable farmland, ancient woods*

SUGGESTED MAP *OS Explorer 180 Oxford, Witney & Woodstock*

START / FINISH *Grid reference: SP 318194*

DOG FRIENDLINESS *Lead essential for road stretches, otherwise excellent*

PARKING *On village street near phone box, Chilson*

PUBLIC TOILETS *None en route*

The Wychwood takes its name from a local Saxon tribe, the Hwicce. At the time of the Norman conquest, Wychwood Forest was one of four royal hunting grounds in England, and covered most of western Oxfordshire. The leafy remains of this once magnificent demesne are now mostly confined to the hilltops that lie between Ascott-under-Wychwood, Charlbury, Ramsden and Leafield, and private land ownership means that access for walkers is sometimes frustratingly limited.

A National Nature Reserve

At its heart is a National Nature Reserve, which preserves some 360 species of wild flowers and ferns, including the elusive yellow star of Bethlehem and the bizarre toothwort, a parasitic plant that is found on the roots of some trees. This walk takes you through the edge of the old woodland, on a path that in spring is carpeted with drifts of bluebells that stretch away as far as you can see. The rich variety of wild flowers means a corresponding abundance of butterflies, including peacock, tortoiseshell and orange tip.

The Shrinking Forest

By 1300 the once-flourishing 'forest' had been split into three sections: Woodstock, based around the royal hunting lodge first built here during the reign of Ethelred II; the area around Cornbury Park; and a section around Witney, where the Bishop of Winchester had built his palace. The forest continued to decline and, by 1857, only 10 square miles (26sq km) were left. As the enclosure of land became commonplace in the 1860s, Kingstanding Farm, passed on this walk, was one of seven new farms built at this time to take advantage of the newly available land.

The Ascott Martyrs

The village of Ascott-under-Wychwood is tucked in the valley below the remnants of the Wychwood, along with its near-neighbours Shipton-under-Wychwood and Milton-under-Wychwood. Ascott may not be the prettiest village, but it has another claim to fame: the Ascott Martyrs. These 16

WYCHWOOD

young women played their part in the Agricultural Revolution of the 19th century when, in 1873, they attempted to dissuade Ramsden men from taking over the jobs of local men, who had been sacked for membership of the Agricultural Workers' Union. Indeed, the women were accused of encouraging the imported labourers to join the same union. Their punishment – imprisonment with hard labour – caused a riot outside the court in Chipping Norton and the women had to be secretly transferred to Oxford gaol. Their sentences were later remitted by Queen Victoria and some accounts say she sent each woman a red flannel petticoat and five shillings. The union presented them with blue silk for dresses and £5 each.

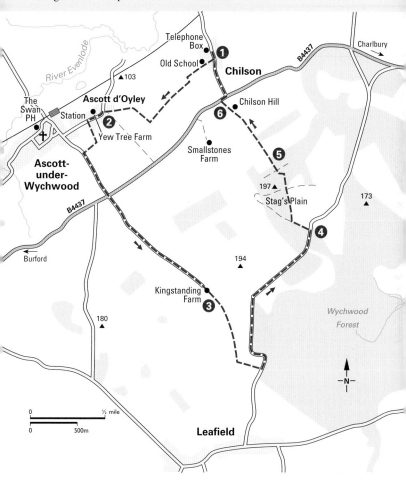

WALK 29 DIRECTIONS

❶ From the phone box, turn south along the village street, and right up School Lane, passing various houses and the Old School at the end, on the right. Follow the bridleway straight on into the field ahead, with the hedge to your right, passing through two gates. Stay on the path round the edge of the field as it kinks left then right. Keep straight on, descend steadily, and follow as the track bends right. At the hedge turn right then immediately left through a gateway; take the track diagonally left across the field (if the track has been ploughed over keep right round the edge of the field) towards Ascott-under-Wychwood, to meet a lane.

2 Turn left along the lane through Ascott d'Oyley, passing Yew Tree Farmhouse on the right. Beyond d'Oyley House and just before a recreation ground turn left up a track, Priory Lane, which becomes a grassy path under trees. It bends sharp right, and emerge at a road by a house. Turn left up the road, and cross the main road at the top with care. Continue straight ahead up the lane, signed

'Restricted byway'. Follow this straight uphill for a mile (1.6km), to pass through the buildings of Kingstanding Farm.

3 Continue down the stony track and keep straight on. It leads along the bottom of a winding, secret valley, with the solid spire of Leafield church up to your right. Emerge at a main road; turn left and follow the road as it snakes uphill, with Wychwood Forest to your right. After about 1 mile (1.6km) the road descends into woodland. As it ascends again, look for a wooden gate on the left, signed 'Circular Walk Footpath'.

4 Turn left through here and follow the track up the edge of

the woods. Keep right and cross the clearing of Stag's Plain. Bend left and right and continue on the track through the woods, carpeted with bluebells in spring.

5 Start to descend and emerge from the woods. Continue straight ahead, following the track downhill, with a hedge on your right. Pass Smallstones Farm, over to the left. Bend left at the bottom of the field, pass a wooden fence, and take the path that leads to the left, down the hill and past Chilson Hill cottage (right).

6 At the bottom of the drive turn right along the main road and immediately left down the road that leads into Chilson village. Enter the village and keep straight on past the tiny triangular green, passing the old Primitive Methodist chapel on your left. Pass the end of School Lane and return to your car.

Walking with Rosie in the Slad Valley

A stroll through the countryside around Slad, backcloth to Laurie Lee's most popular novel.

DISTANCE *3.75 miles (6km)*   **MINIMUM TIME** *2hrs*

ASCENT/GRADIENT *425ft (130m)* ▲▲▲   **LEVEL OF DIFFICULTY** ✚✚✚

PATHS *Tracks, fields and quiet lanes, 17 stiles*

LANDSCAPE *Hills, valleys and woodland*

SUGGESTED MAP *OS Explorer 179 Gloucester, Cheltenham & Stroud*

START / FINISH *Grid reference: SO 878087*

DOG FRIENDLINESS *Mostly off lead – livestock encountered occasionally*

PARKING *Lay-by at Bull's Cross*

PUBLIC TOILETS *None en route*

The Slad Valley is one of the least spoiled parts of the Cotswolds, notwithstanding its invariable association with the area's most important literary figure, the poet Laurie Lee (1914–97). And yet he is not instantly remembered for his poetry but for *Cider With Rosie* (1959). This autobiographical account of a Cotswold childhood has, for thousands of students, been part of their English Literature syllabus.

A Childhood Gone Forever

For anyone coming to the area, *Cider With Rosie* is well worth reading, but it is especially pertinent here as it is largely set in Slad, where Lee was brought up and lived for much of his life. The book charts, in poetic language, the experiences of a child living in a world that is within living memory and yet has quite disappeared. Some of the episodes recounted in the book are said to have been products of Lee's imagination but, as he said himself, it was the 'feeling' of his childhood that he was endeavouring to capture.

A Spanish Odyssey

The story of his life is, anyway, an interesting one. He spent a considerable time in Spain and became involved in the Spanish Civil War and the struggle against Franco. Afterwards he established a reputation as a poet, mixing with the literati of the day. He was never very prolific – much of his energy appears to have been poured into love affairs. He did, however, write plays for radio and was involved in film-making during the Second World War. But it was with the publication of *Cider With Rosie* that he became a household name. Readers from all over the world identified with his magical evocation of rural English life and the book has not been out of print since. To some extent Lee became a prisoner of a *Cider With Rosie* industry. The picture of an avuncular figure living a bucolic idyll was not a strictly accurate one – much of his time was spent in London. He was susceptible to illness all his life. Nonetheless, in his later years he managed to complete his autobiographical trilogy. His second volume, *As I Walked Out One Midsummer Morning* (1969) describes his journey from Gloucestershire

SLAD VALLEY

to Spain as an itinerant fiddle player. The third, *A Moment of War* (1991), recounts his experiences there during the Civil War. Lee died in 1997 and is buried in Slad churchyard. Many of the places in and around the village mentioned in *Cider With Rosie* are readily identifiable today. Although it is no longer possible to frolic in the roads with impunity, the valley remains as beautiful as it ever was.

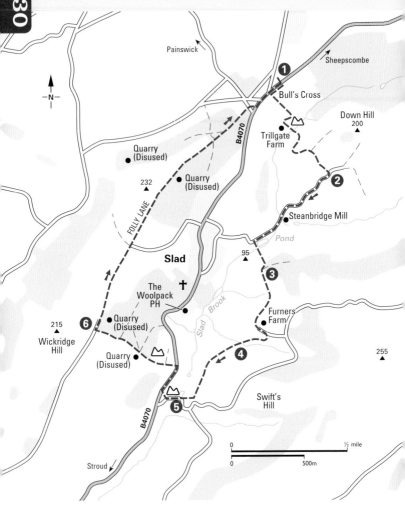

WALK 30 DIRECTIONS

1 From Bull's Cross walk to the south end of the lay-by and turn left on to a tarmac-covered footpath, the Wysis Way. Follow it down and, immediately before Trillgate Farm turn left over a stile into a field. Go half right, down the field and up the other

side, to a gate and stile at the top. Turn left along a track. Where it joins another track stay right and continue to a lane.

2 Turn right and walk to the bottom. Pass Steanbridge Mill and if you want to visit Slad, follow the lane into the village. To continue the walk turn left immediately after the large pond along a restricted byway and walk to a stile. Cross into a field, with a hedge on your right, and continue to a stile at the top.

3 Cross and follow a path to another stile. Follow the left side of the next field and go over another stile, then continue along the path. Pass through a gate on to a track, stay to the right of Furners Farm and curve left. About 30yds (27m) after the curve turn right over a stile on to a wooded path and after 130yds (118m) go right again over a stile into a field. Walk ahead, with the farm above you and to the right. Cross another stile and then keep to the right of a small pond.

4 At the top of the pond cross a stile into a field. Go half left across it to a gate and stile. In the next field head straight across its lower part. At a point where a telegraph pole stands close to a hedge, turn right over a stile on to a track. Turn left to meet a lane.

5 Turn right and follow the lane to the valley bottom. Start to climb the other side and at a corner go over a stile on your right by The Vatch Cottage. Ascend steeply, skirting the garden, to another stile at the road. Turn right along the pavement. After 150yds (137m) bear left on to a public footpath and climb steeply. At a junction of footpaths bear left and continue to a field. Follow the margin of the field up to a stile, then follow the path as it weaves between a dry-stone wall and the edge of woodland.

6 At the top go over a stile, turn right on to Folly Lane and continue to a junction. If you want to go into Slad, turn right, otherwise continue ahead on to a path that will soon take you through the Frith Wood Nature Reserve. Walk through the woods, finally emerging at your starting point at Bull's Cross.

Uley and its Magnificent Fort on the Hill

The vast bulk of the ancient fort of Uley Bury forms the centrepiece for this walk along the Cotswold escarpment.

DISTANCE *3 miles (4.8km)*   MINIMUM TIME *1hr 30min*

ASCENT/GRADIENT *345ft (105m)* ▲▲▲   LEVEL OF DIFFICULTY ✦✦✦

PATHS *Tracks and fields*

LANDSCAPE *Valley, meadows, woodland and open hilltop*

SUGGESTED MAP *OS Explorer 168 Stroud, Tetbury & Malmesbury*

START / FINISH *Grid reference: ST 789984*

DOG FRIENDLINESS *Suitable in parts but livestock on Uley Bury and in fields on extension to Owlpen*

PARKING *Main street of Uley*

PUBLIC TOILETS *None en route*

Uley is a pretty village, strung along a wide street at the foot of a high, steep hill. It is distinctive for several reasons. It has its own brewery, which produces some fine beers including Uley Bitter and Uley Old Spot. In the past the village specialised in the production of 'Uley Blue' cloth, which was used in military uniforms. And then there is Uley Bury, dating back to the Iron Age and one of the finest hill-forts in the Cotswolds.

Peaceful Settlements

There are many hundreds of Iron Age forts throughout England and Wales. They are concentrated in Cornwall, South West Wales and the Welsh Marches, with secondary concentrations throughout the Cotswolds, North Wales and Wessex. Although the term 'hill-fort' is generally used in connection with these settlements, the term can be misleading. There are many that were built on level ground and there are many that were not used purely for military purposes – often they were simply settlements located on easily-defended sites. Broadly speaking, there are five types, classified according to the nature of the site on which they were built, rather than, say, the date of their construction. Contour forts were built more or less along the perimeter edge of a hilltop; promontory forts were built on a spur, surrounded by natural defences on two or more sides; valley and plateau forts (two types) depended heavily on artificial defences and were located, as their names suggest, in valleys or on flat land respectively; and multiple-enclosure forts were usually built in a poor strategic position on the slope of a hill and were perhaps used as stockades.

Natural Defences

Uley Bury, covering about 38 acres (15.4ha), is classified as an inland promontory fort and was built in the 6th century BC. It falls away on three sides, the fourth side, which faces away from the escarpment, is protected by specially constructed ramparts which would have been surmounted by a wooden palisade. The natural defences – that is, the Cotswold escarpment, facing west – were also strengthened by the construction of a wide and deep ditch, as well as two additional ramparts, an inner one and an outer one, between which the footpath largely threads its course. The three main entrances were at the northern, eastern and southern corners. These, vulnerable parts of the fort, would have been fortified with log barriers.

Although some tribespeople would have lived permanently in huts within the fort, most would have lived outside, either on other parts of the hill or in the valleys below. In an emergency, therefore, there was space for those who lived outside the fort to take shelter within. Eventually the fort was taken over by the Dobunni tribe – Celtic interlopers from mainland Europe who arrived about 100 BC – and appears to have been occupied by them throughout the Roman era.

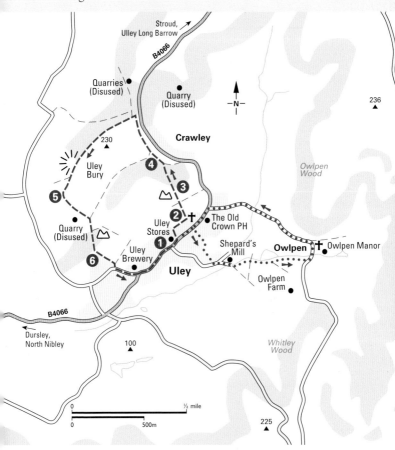

WALK 31 DIRECTIONS

❶ From the main street locate the Uley Stores (on your left as you walk up the street). Walk along the narrow lane (to the right, as you look at the stores). Pass between houses as the lane

dwindles to a track. Some 13yds (12m) before a stile turn right along a public footpath towards the church.

❷ When the churchyard can be seen on the right, turn left up a narrow path beside a cottage. This

rises fairly sharply and brings you to a kissing gate. Pass through into a meadow. Climb steeply up the grassland towards woodland.

❸ At the treeline keep left of the woods. In a corner on the far left go through a gate and follow a winding woodland path uphill. When you come to a fence stay on the path as it bears left. Pass through a gate and continue uphill, to exit the woods. In 40yds (37m) bear left as the path rises across grassland to a junction.

❹ Turn right to follow the contour of the hill – the edge of the ancient fort. You are following the perimeter of the fort in an anti-clockwise direction, with steep drops to your right. Pass through a gate, meeting a junction of paths. Go left along the edge of the hill, with views to the west, disregarding a stile to your right that invites you to descend.

❺ At the next corner go through a gate and continue to follow the edge of the fort. At the next corner, at the fort's south-eastern point, bear right on a bridleway that descends through hillocks. Pass go through a gate and continue dropping steeply through bushes, keeping left. This will bring you to a gate into a meadow and the access path to Whitecourt underground reservoir.

❻ Walk along the path, all the way to a cottage and then a kissing gate. Go through this and pass beside the cottage to arrive at a lane. Turn left here and follow the lane, soon passing the Uley Brewery, to reach the main road. Turn left, passing South Street, to return to the start.

EXTENDING THE WALK

Owlpen Manor is well worth a visit. Walk down Woodstock Terrace, opposite the church, to South Street and turn left. Go right by Shepard's Mill and, at the stile by the river, turn left and walk  through three fields to reach Owlpen Manor. You can return to Uley on the road or retrace your steps.

Weaving Along the Stroud Valley

Discover the impact of the Industrial Revolution in the Cotswold valleys.

DISTANCE *6 miles (9.7km)*   **MINIMUM TIME** *3hrs*

ASCENT/GRADIENT *495ft (150m)* ▲▲▲   **LEVEL OF DIFFICULTY** ✦✦✦

PATHS *Fields, lanes, canal path and tracks, 3 stiles*

LANDSCAPE *Canal, road and railway, valley and steep slopes, villages*

SUGGESTED MAP *OS Explorer 168 Stroud, Tetbury & Malmesbury*

START / FINISH *Grid reference: SO 892025*

DOG FRIENDLINESS *Good, with few stiles and little livestock*

PARKING *Lay-by east of Chalford church*

PUBLIC TOILETS *None en route*

Wool has been associated with the Cotswolds for centuries. During the Middle Ages the fleece of the 'Cotswold Lion' breed was the most prized in all of Europe. Merchants from many countries despatched their agents to purchase it from the fairs and markets of the wold towns in the northern part of the region – most famously Northleach, Cirencester and Chipping Campden. Woven cloth eventually became a more important export and so the industry moved to the southern Cotswolds, whose valleys and faster-flowing streams, which were suited to powering woollen mills.

Mechanisation

The concentration of mills in the Stroud area was evident by the early 15th century. Indeed, its importance was such that when a 1557 Act of Parliament restricted cloth manufacture to towns, the villages of the Stroud area were exempted. By 1700 the lower Stroud Valley was producing about 4.59 million square metres of cloth every year. At this time the spinning and weaving was done in domestic dwellings or workhouses, the woven cloth then being returned to the mill for finishing. The Industrial Revolution was to bring rapid change. There was great opposition to the introduction of mechanical spinning and shearing machines. This was heightened in 1795 by the development of the improved broadloom with its flying shuttle. The expectation was that, as well as compelling weavers to work in the mills, it would bring mass unemployment. Progress marched on, however, and by the mid-19th century there were over 1,000 looms at work in the Stroud Valley. They came with their share of political unrest too, and in 1825 and 1828 strikes and riots broke out. The industry went into decline as steam replaced water power and it migrated northwards to the Pennines. By 1901 only 3,000 people were employed in the cloth industry, compared with 24,000 in the mid-17th century. Today, only one mill remains.

Graceful Elevations

This walk begins in Chalford, an attractive village built on the steep sides of the Stroud Valley. Its streets are lined with 18th- and 19th-century clothiers' terraces and weavers' cottages. On the canalside the shells of woollen mills are still plentiful.

The 18th-century church contains fine examples of craftsmanship from the Arts and Crafts period of the late 19th century. Nether Lypiatt Manor is a handsome manor house now owned by Prince and Princess Michael of Kent. Known locally as 'the haunted house', it was built in 1702 for Judge Charles Cox. Its classical features and estate railings, all unusual in the Cotswolds, inspired wealthy clothiers to spend their money on the addition of graceful elevations to their own houses.

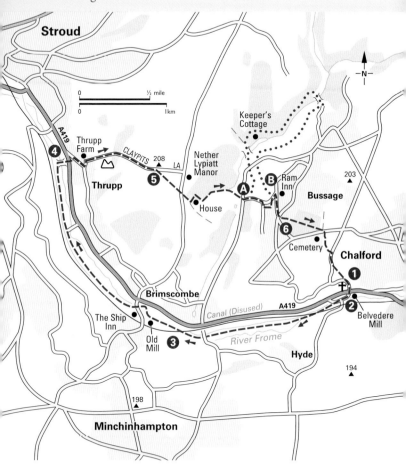

WALK 32 DIRECTIONS

❶ Walk towards Chalford church. Immediately before it, cross the road and locate a path going right, towards a canal roundhouse. Note the Belvedere Mill across to your left and follow the tow path alongside the Thames and Severn Canal on your right.

❷ Cross a road and continue along the tow path as it descends steps. Now follow this path for about 2 miles (3.2km). It will soon disappear under the railway line via a gloomy culvert, so that the railway will now be on your right, beyond the old canal. Old mills and small factories line the route.

❸ Shortly before arriving in Brimscombe the tow path passes beneath the railway again and continues past a restored mill. Soon after, it becomes a road leading into an industrial estate. At a road opposite a large mill, Brimscombe Port Old Mill, turn left, to come to a junction. Cross and turn right. Immediately after The Ship Inn turn left along a road among offices and workshops. Continue straight on along a path, with factory walls to your right. The canal reappears on your left. As you walk on into the country you will pass beneath two brick bridges and a metal footbridge.

❹ At the next bridge, with a hamlet on your left, turn right to follow a track via two bridges to a road. Cross this and turn left. After 50 paces turn right up a short path to meet Thrupp Lane. Turn right, and at the top, turn left. Turn right just before Thrupp Farm into Claypits Lane and climb up steeply.

❺ After a long climb, as the road levels out, you will see Nether Lypiatt Manor in front of you. Turn right, beside a sycamore tree, over a stile into a field. Go half left to the far corner. Cross a stone stile and follow a narrow path beside trees to a road.

Descend a lane opposite. Where it appears to fork, go straight on, then hairpin left to descend past a house. Enter woodland and fork right near the bottom. Keep a pond on your left and cross a road to climb Bussage Hill. After 100yds (91m) pass a lane on the left. At the top turn left opposite the church lychgate on to a path which becomes a lane. Opposite the Ram Inn turn right.

❻ After a telephone box and bus shelter turn left to follow a path among houses into woodland. Go ahead until you meet a road. Turn left and immediately right down a path beside a cemetery. Descend to another road. Turn right for 150yds (137m), then turn left down a steep lane among trees, leading back to Chalford. At the bottom turn left to return to the start of the walk.

EXTENDING THE WALK

Between points **❺** and **❻** you descend into the Toadsmoor Valley, one of the less accessible Cotswold valleys. You can make an interesting detour up the valley, which has fine woodland and a pond, from Point **Ⓐ**, returning to the main route at Point **Ⓑ** near the Ram Inn.

Spring Fashions – Dressing Bisley's Wells

From beautiful Bisley, this ramble follows undulating field paths taking in small villages and hamlets along the way.

DISTANCE 5.5 miles (8.8km) **MINIMUM TIME** 2hrs 30min

ASCENT/GRADIENT 150ft (46m) ▲▲▲ **LEVEL OF DIFFICULTY** ✚✚✚

PATHS Tracks, fields, lanes, 19 stiles

LANDSCAPE Secluded valleys, villages, open wold

SUGGESTED MAP OS Explorer 168 Stroud, Tetbury & Malmesbury

START / FINISH Grid reference: SO 903060

DOG FRIENDLINESS Quite good – little livestock

PARKING In Bisley village near The Bear Inn

PUBLIC TOILETS None en route

There are many beautiful villages in the Cotswolds and this walk takes you to one of the loveliest. Bisley is well known in the area for its well-dressing ceremony which takes place on Ascension Day – a Thursday 40 days after Easter. This tradition, usually associated with the Peak District where wells have been dressed for centuries, was originally a pagan ceremony. But in the 14th century it became a thanksgiving for wells that remained uncontaminated during the Black Death. In Bisley village the tradition dates from the restoration of the wells in Wells Street in 1863 by the Revd Thomas Keble – the vicar of Bisley at the time and the younger brother of John Keble (1792–1866) the poet, theologian and founder of Keble College in Oxford.

Keeping Traditions Alive

The problem of keeping such traditions alive are twofold – fostering local enthusiasm and, in this case, obtaining the necessary funds for the children's refreshments and for paying the brass band. Moss and flowers are collected to cover the frames and hoops carried by 22 children from the local Bluecoat school in the procession to the wells. In the past all of this was done in grat secrecy, in the spirit of competition, while these days most of the decorative work is done in school. Another problem is finding enough flowers at this time of year and keeping them fresh enough to use in the ceremony.

On Ascension Day itself, a service is held in the parish church, then the children's procession forms; the oldest children have the privilege of carrying the largest floral stars at the front. The procession, preceded by the band and the vicar, marches through the village down to the wells where the vicar performs a short blessing. The flowers are arranged by the children to spell 'Ascension' and 'AD' and the current year, while garlands, floral hoops, and Stars of David are laid about the wells. A hymn is sung and the children sit down to a tea. Finally, in the late afternoon, there are village sports, such as egg and spoon and sack races.

BISLEY

Remarkable Village

Bisley is remarkable in a number of ways. In the churchyard is a 13th-century Poor Soul's Light, the only outdoor example in the country. It was used to light Mass candles on behalf of those who were too poor to buy their own. And then there is the Bisley Boy. Legend says that the real Queen Elizabeth I is buried in Bisley churchyard. During a visit here as a girl, apparently, she fell ill and died. A local boy who closely resembled her took her place and went on to become Queen…

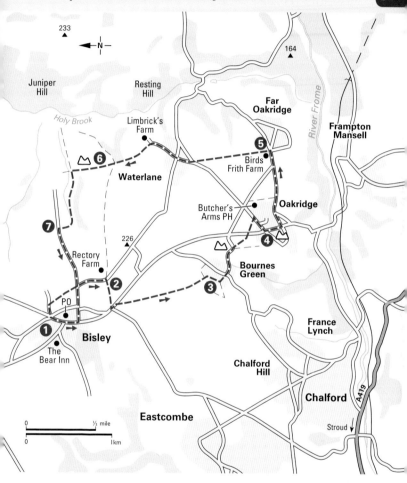

WALK 33 DIRECTIONS

❶ From your parking spot in Bisley village walk down to the main street, opposite the post office. Turn right and take the first turn left up a street to a junction. Go straight on, signposted 'Waterlane', and then follow this as it goes sharply to the right.

❷ After 400yds (366m), opposite Rectory Farm, turn right through a gate and walk through a gate and two fields to a road. Through a gate, cross to a stile to the left of a stone stable and then a paddock to another stile. Go half right across two fields via two stiles and then half right to a gap in the hedge and along the field margin to a hedge

BISLEY

WALK 33

WHILE YOU'RE THERE

Cirencester is a town of great interest. Cirencester Park, partly designed by the poet Alexander Pope for the first Lord Bathurst, is a frequent venue for polo tournaments. The Corinium Museum is excellent and on the main square is the largest parish church in England.

gap in the corner. Turn half left across the field to a stile in the corner and head for the stile at the tree edge. Descend a path through the trees to a small field. Go half right to cross a track and a stile. Cross to a path beside houses and descend left into Bournes Green via a stile, turning left soon after.

❸ Turn right to reach a junction and turn left. At the next junction, descend straight across to a lane via a grassy bank, passing a seat. Follow this lane steeply down across a stream and uphill to a hairpin bend opposite a cottage with a conservatory. Turn right over a stile and go immediately left through a bank of trees to a double stile. Continue half right across the field to a stile on to a road. Cross the road to enter another field via a stile. Across the field, go over a stile and turn right on to a road.

WHERE TO EAT AND DRINK

In Oakridge the Butcher's Arms is on the walk while there are two pubs in Bisley, both of which are good, comfortable locals. The Bear Inn on George Street has its origins as a building in the 16th century and has been a pub since 1766. It serves traditional British food and dogs and children are welcome. The Stirrup Cup also serves food along with Hook Norton and Wadworth's ales.

❹ Take the second lane on the left which descends steeply (signposted 'Frampton Marshall') and turn left beyond the stone water pump and war memorial, signed 'Oakridge'. Follow this lane as it bears right at 'Whitespring' house and up and out of the village.

❺ After about 0.5 mile (800m), at a crossroads at Fair Oakridge, turn left on to a track to the right of Birds Frith Farm. At the end continue down to a junction at Waterlane. Take the leftmost of the two lanes here and drop to a crossroads. Go straight on (signed 'No Through Road'). At a farm bear left on to a track and follow this to a gate, past a spinney.

WHAT TO LOOK OUT FOR

In Bisley look for the impressive semi-circular building which houses the famous well.

❻ Through this go straight on uphill to the crest of the field and on to a stile in woodland. Follow a steep footpath down to a stile. Descend a field, turning left before you reach the bottom. Walk through fields alongside a stream and ponds, crossing two stiles, and then bear right well before a gate. At a guide post. Cross the stream (no bridge) and walk uphill along the edge of a wood to a stile at the crest.

❼ Turn left and walk all the way to a junction. Turn right along a track and enter a field via a kissing gate. Go half left to the other side through a kissing gate and then left along a footpath to a road. Cross the road (watch out for traffic here as it can be busy) and descend some steps to central Bisley, and the start.

Sapperton and the Thames & Severn Canal

Sapperton, both the focus of a major engineering project and a cradle for cultural change.

DISTANCE 6 miles (9.7km)   **MINIMUM TIME** 3hrs

ASCENT/GRADIENT 345ft (105m) ▲▲▲   **LEVEL OF DIFFICULTY** ✦✦✦

PATHS Woodland paths and tracks, fields, lanes and canalside paths, 18 stiles

LANDSCAPE Secluded valleys and villages

SUGGESTED MAP OS Explorer 168 Stroud, Tetbury & Malmesbury

START / FINISH Grid reference: SO 948033

DOG FRIENDLINESS Good – very few livestock

PARKING In Sapperton village near church

PUBLIC TOILETS None en route

Sapperton was at the centre of two conflicting tendencies during the late 18th and early 20th centuries – the Industrial Revolution and the Romantic Revival. In the first case, it was canal technology that came to Sapperton. Canal construction was widespread throughout England from the mid-18th century onwards. Just as 'dot com' companies attracted vast sums of money in the late 1990s, so investors poured their money into 18th-century joint stock companies, regardless of their profitability. Confidence was high and investors expected to reap the rewards of commercial success based on the need to ship goods swiftly across the country.

Tunnel Vision

One key project was thought to be the canal that would link the River Severn and the River Thames. The main obstacle was the need for a tunnel through the Cotswolds, the cost of which could be unpredictable. But these were heady days and investors' money was forthcoming to press ahead with the scheme in 1783. During the tunnel's construction, the diarist and traveller John Byng visited the workings. With obvious distaste he wrote, 'I was enveloped in thick smoke arising from the gunpowder of the miners, at whom, after passing by many labourers who work by small candles, I did at last arrive; they come from the Derbyshire and Cornish mines, are in eternal danger and frequently perish by falls of earth.'

Legwork

The Thames and Severn Canal opened in 1789, linking the Thames at Lechlade with the Stroudwater Navigation at Stroud. The Sapperton Tunnel, at 3,400yds (3,109m) long, is still one of the longest transport tunnels in the country. Barges were propelled through the tunnel by means of 'leggers', who 'walked' against the tunnel walls and who patronised the inns that are at both tunnel entrances. Yet the canal was not a success: either there was too much or too little water; rock falls and leakages required constant attention. The cost of maintaining the tunnel led to the closure of the canal in 1911.

SAPPERTON

The Arts and Crafts Movement

It isn't just the great canal tunnel that is of interest in Sapperton. Some of the cottages here were built by disciples of William Morris (1834–96). He was the doyen of the Arts and Crafts Movement in design. It aspired to reintroduce to English life a simple yet decorative functionality, in part as a reaction to the growing mass-production methods engendered by the Industrial Revolution. Furniture makers and architects like Ernest Gimson (from Leicestershire), Sidney and Ernest Barnsley (from Birmingham), and Norman Jewson, all worked in Daneway, at Daneway House. Gimson and the Barnsley brothers are buried at Sapperton church.

You'll find the finest example of the Arts and Crafts vernacular-style architecture in Sapperton is Upper Dorval House. The entrance to the western end of the Sapperton Tunnel is in fact in the hamlet of Daneway, a short walk along the path from the Daneway Inn, which was formerly called the Bricklayer's Arms. Daneway House, the 14th-century house that was let to followers of William Morris by Earl Bathurst, is a short distance up the road from the pub.

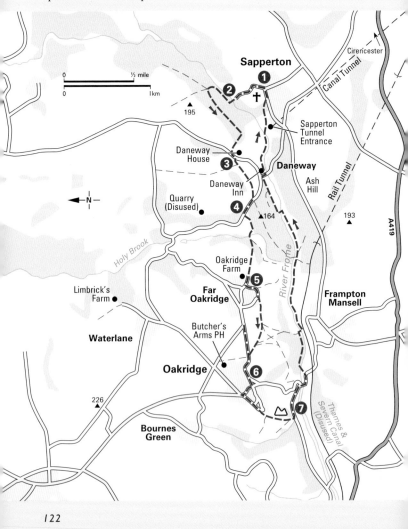

WALK 34 DIRECTIONS

1 With the church to your left, walk along a 'No Through Road'. This descends rapidly and, by the entrance to a house at the bottom, turn left on to a footpath. This turns right and into woodland

2 Cross a stream and continue left uphill into woodland. Take the main path and, where it forks, go left uphill. Climb to a junction of tracks. Turn left at the guide post and stay on the track mainly in woodland for 0.5 mile (800m) to a gate at a lane.

3 Turn left and then immediately right over a stile (opposite Daneway House). Cross another stile and walk along a wide grassy area, with a fence to the right, to a kissing gate at a lane. Turn right for 250yds (229m) then turn left over a stile.

4 Walk down a drive. Just before the house go left through a hedge and turn immediately right, following a path to a gate. Cross this, then a stile and bridge, a field, and a stile into woodland. Follow a path to a stile at a field and cross half right, heading for farm buildings. Pass through a gate and go left of Oakridge Farm to a stile on to a lane.

5 Turn left and pass a junction, signed 'Trillis'. At a sharp right corner go ahead into a field. Walk to a stile at the far end. Cross the next field and find a stile in the top right corner. Go straight ahead to follow the left margin of the next field to a stile at a road. Turn left along the road to descend through Oakridge.

6 At bottom of the hill, the road bears left, then take the right fork uphill. At a crossroads turn right, climbing steeply to a junction. Turn left. At the village green go to its end and bear right to a stile. Enter a field, keep close to a hedgerow on the left-hand side and cross three further stiles. Bear right across a field to a stile into woodland. Soon, over another stile, descend steeply and turn left on to a footpath, which you follow to a junction. Turn left down to reach a road.

7 Turn left then, at a junction, turn right to cross a bridge. Bear left and after 50 paces turn left again over a footbridge with a stile at each end, then right on to a footpath, the canal tow path. Follow the canal for 600yds (549m) with one kissing gate. Go right across the canal bridge and turn left back on to the canal tow path for 1.5 miles (2.4km), passing through three kissing gates and over a modern footbridge, to reach a road by the Daneway Inn. Turn right over a bridge and then left to continue by the canal. Cross over one stile to the Sapperton Tunnel. Walk above the tunnel's portico to a field. Over a stile bear half right up to a kissing gate. Go left on to a path and walk up to a lane which leads back into Sapperton. Turn left and then right at the churchyard to return to the start.

The Woven Charm of Bibury

The outer charm of a weavers' village conceals miserable workings conditions.

DISTANCE 6.25 miles (10.1km)   MINIMUM TIME 2hrs 30min

ASCENT/GRADIENT 165ft (50m) ▲▲▲   LEVEL OF DIFFICULTY +++

PATHS *Fields, tracks and lane, may be muddy in places, 5 stiles*

LANDSCAPE *Exposed wolds, valley, villages and streams*

SUGGESTED MAP *OS Explorer OL45 The Cotswolds*

START / FINISH *Grid reference: SP 113068*

DOG FRIENDLINESS *On lead throughout – a lot of sheep and horses*

PARKING *Bibury village*

PUBLIC TOILETS *Opposite river on main street, close to Arlington Row*

Arlington Row is the picturesque terrace of cottages that led William Morris to refer to Bibury as the most beautiful village in England. It was originally built, it is thought, in the late 14th century, to house sheep belonging to Osney Abbey in Oxford. The wool was washed in the river and then hung out to dry on Rack Isle, the marshy area in front of the cottages. Following the Dissolution of the Monasteries the land was sold off and the sheep houses converted to weavers' cottages. Before mechanisation transformed the wool weaving industry, most weaving took place in the houses of the poor. Firstly, women and children spun the wool either at home or at the workhouse. Then it was transferred to the houses of the weavers, who worked on handlooms at home at piece rates.

A typical weaver's cottage might have had four rooms, with a kitchen and workshop downstairs and a bedroom and storeroom upstairs. There were very few items of furniture in the living rooms, while the workroom would have contained little more than a broadloom and the appropriate tools. The woven cloth was then returned to the clothier's mill for fulling and cutting. Work on cloth was often a condition of tenure imposed by landlords. The merchant landlord fixed a piecework rate and, provided that the work was satisfactory, the cottage could stay in the weaver's family from generation to generation. Weaving went on this way for some 200 years, until the introduction of steam power in the 18th century, after which it tended to take place in the Stroud Valley mills. Despite their unfavourable conditions, the cottage weavers resisted the change but to no avail.

Strictly speaking, much of what is considered picturesque in Bibury is in the neighbouring village of Arlington, but they are now indistinguishable. Apart from Arlington Row, there is plenty to enjoy in the village, especially the church, which has Saxon origins and is set in pretty gardens. Across the bridge is the old mill, open to the public. Nearby Ablington has an enchanting group of cottages, threaded by the River Coln. *A Cotswold Village* (1898), which describes local life in the late 19th century, was written by J Arthur Gibbs who lived at Ablington Manor. You pass the walls of the manor on the walk. In the village, are a couple of 18th-century barns.

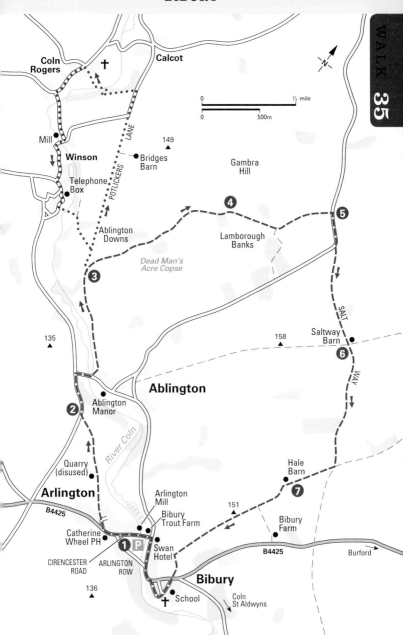

WALK 35

WALK 35 DIRECTIONS

❶ From the parking area opposite Arlington Mill, walk along the Cirencester road, away from Bibury. Opposite the telephone box after the Catherine

Wheel pub turn right along a lane and then keep left at a fork. Pass some cottages and go through a gate and two stiles into a field. Walk on the same line across stiles and fields until you pass to the right of a house to a road.

2 Turn right and walk down to a junction. Turn right into Ablington and cross the River Colne bridge. After 60 paces, turn left along a track with houses on your right and a stream to your left. Continue to a gate and then follow the track, arriving at another gate after 0.5 mile (800m).

3 Go into a field and turn sharp right along the valley bottom. Follow a twisting route along the bottom of the valley. When you reach the next gate continue into a field, still following the contours of the valley. The route will eventually take you through a gate, at the far end of the field beyond pollarded ash trees, just before a barn and another gate immediately after.

4 Keep to the track as it bears into the right-hand valley and gently ascends a long slope, with woodland to your left. When the track goes sharp right just beyond the end of a conifer plantation, with a gate before you, turn left through a gate on to a track. Follow it all the way to a road.

5 Through a gate turn right. After 250yds (229m), where the road goes right, continue straight on, to enter a track (the Salt Way). Continue along this via a gate for over 0.5 mile (800m), until you reach the remains of Saltway Barn.

6 Do not walk ahead but, immediately after the barns, turn left into a field and then right

WHERE TO EAT AND DRINK

The Catherine Wheel is a pleasant pub on the Cirencester road, just beyond the mill. The Swan Hotel has a good restaurant and also serves teas. Snacks are available at Bibury Trout Farm and at the mill.

along its right-hand margin. Walk on for just under 0.75 mile (1.2km), passing hedge and woodland and, where the track breaks to the right, turn right through a gate in a stone field wall into a field; keep the wall on your right.

7 Walk on to pass to the left of Hale Barn after a gate. Enter a track, with the large buildings of Bibury Farm away to your left, and keep on the same line through gates where they arise. Eventually reaching cottages, you will descend to a drive which will, in turn, bring you to a road in Bibury. Cross the road to walk down between a row of cottages. At the end, near the church and school, turn right. Walk along the pavement into the village, passing Arlington Row and the river on your left.

EXTENDING THE WALK

You can extend the walk up the Coln Valley to Winson and Coln Rogers by leaving the main route at Point **3** to continue on Potlickers Lane. Cross the river and return along the road through the villages until a path brings you back to Point **3** where you can continue the main walk. Note that in heavy rain Coln Rogers can be seriously flooded.

Burford – a Classic Cotswold Town

Discover the delights of an ancient settlement with a long history on this attractive walk through the Windrush Valley.

DISTANCE *5 miles (8km)*   MINIMUM TIME *2hrs 30min*

ASCENT/GRADIENT *250ft (76m)* ▲▲▲   LEVEL OF DIFFICULTY ✦✦✦

PATHS *Field and riverside paths, tracks, country roads, 7 stiles*

LANDSCAPE *Undulating Windrush Valley to the east of Burford*

SUGGESTED MAP *OS Explorer OL45 The Cotswolds*

START / FINISH *Grid reference: SP 255123*

DOG FRIENDLINESS *Under control across farmland; on lead where requested*

PARKING *Large car park to east of Windrush, near parish church*

PUBLIC TOILETS *Burford High Street*

Often described as the gateway to the Cotswolds, the picturesque town of Burford has changed little over the years. The High Street runs down between lime trees and mellow stone houses to a narrow three-arched bridge over the River Windrush. Charles II and his mistress Nell Gwynn, whose child was named the Earl of Burford, attended Burford races and stayed at the George Hotel. When she retired to Windsor, Gwynn called her home there Burford House.

An Important Trading Centre

Situated at several major east–west and north–south crossing routes, Burford has always been regarded as an important trading centre. People would pay their tolls at the twin-gabled 15th-century Tolsey, now a museum, for the right to trade in the town and it was here that the prosperous Guild of Merchants conducted their meetings. Such was their power and influence that by the Middle Ages the merchants were running Burford as if it boasted a Mayor and Corporation.

Take a leisurely stroll through the streets of the town and you'll stumble across a host of treasures – especially in the little side roads leading off the High Street. For example, the Great House in Witney Street was the largest residence in Burford when it was built about 1690. With its Georgian façade, it certainly dwarfs the other buildings in the street. The Dolls' House, dating back to 1939 and on view in the Tolsey Museum, is modelled on the Great House.

A Gem of a Church

Burford's parish church, with its slender spire, is one of the largest in Oxfordshire. Begun about 1170, it was enlarged over subsequent centuries and one of its last additions was the south porch, noted for its elaborate stonework. The west doorway is pure Norman, as is the central part of the tower, to which another stage was added in the 15th century to provide a base for the spire. Inside, the ceiling is fan vaulted and there are five medieval screens dividing various chapels.

Levellers Revolt

This sizeable wool church is also associated with the Civil War Levellers – 800 Parliamentarian troopers who mutinied at Salisbury over pay and then marched north to join forces with other groups. On 14 May 1649 they reached Burford where they believed they would negotiate a settlement with Fairfax, the Commander-in-Chief. However, Fairfax had different plans and at midnight he and Cromwell entered the town with 2,000 horsemen. Following a skirmish, they captured 340 men. The prisoners were held in the church where one of them carved his name on the font. Two days later, on 17 May, three ringleaders were shot in the churchyard and a fourth was forced to preach a sermon.

Speaker's House

The Priory in Priory Lane is another of Burford's historic buildings. This Elizabethan house, rebuilt in the early 1800s, still has its Tudor gables and the heraldic arms over the doorway recall William Lenthall (1591–1662) who lived here and was elected Speaker to the Long Parliament in 1640.

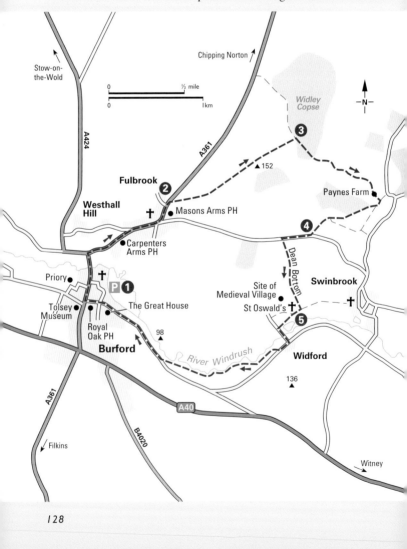

WALK 36 DIRECTIONS

❶ Head north along the High Street to the Windrush. Cross the river and turn right at the mini-roundabout towards Fulbrook. Pass the Carpenters Arms and continue along the road. Avoid a turning for Swinbrook and pass the Masons Arms. Keep ahead, passing Upper End on the left, and look for a footpath on the right.

❷ Follow the steps cut into the side of the slope up to the field-edge and then swing right. Follow the boundary to a waymark just before a slope and curve left to cross the field. Go through a gap in the hedge on the far side and cross the field to an opening in the hedgerow. Cross the next field towards a curtain of woodland and make for a track.

WHERE TO EAT AND DRINK

Burford has plenty of places to eat and drink – from hotel restaurants to pub food and tea shops. Just at the end of the walk is the Royal Oak which serves coffee and tea, as well as toasted teacakes. Various specials, snacks and ploughman's lunches are also available.

❸ Keep right and follow the track through the woodland. Break cover from the trees and pass a row of cottages. Continue down the track to Paynes Farm and, just beyond it, turn right to join a signposted right of way. Head for a gate and follow the unfenced track towards trees. Descend the slope to a gate and continue ahead between hedges up the hill to the road.

❹ Turn right and follow the road down into a dip. Swing left at the stile and sign for Widford

and follow the grassy ride through verdant Dean Bottom. Make for a stile, turn right when you reach the T-junction and visit Widford's St Oswald's Church.

WHAT TO LOOK OUT FOR

The little medieval Church of St Oswald, built on the site of a Roman villa, includes a mosaic floor near the altar, discovered in 1904. Near by is the abandoned site of a medieval village; imagine the slopes of the valley crowded at one time with houses.

❺ On leaving the church, veer right and follow the grassy track, passing a lake on the left. Turn left at the road, recross the Windrush and turn right at the junction. Keep to the road until you reach a footpath sign and stile on the right. Follow the riverside path across a series of stiles, to eventually reach the road. Turn right towards Burford, pass the Great House and the Royal Oak and return to the High Street.

WHILE YOU'RE THERE

Visit the nearby village of Filkins, home to the Swinford Museum which illustrates west Oxfordshire's rural heritage. The village boasts a Victorian church built in the French Gothic style and was once the home of Sir Stafford Cripps, Chancellor of the Exchequer (1947–50) in the post-war Labour cabinet.

Mysteries at Minster Lovell

A gentle stroll through meadows and woods beside the Windrush.

DISTANCE 4 miles (6.4km)   **MINIMUM TIME** 1hr 30min

ASCENT/GRADIENT 180ft (55m) ▲▲▲   **LEVEL OF DIFFICULTY** ✦✦✦

PATHS Meadows, tracks, pavement and lane, woodland, 2 stiles

LANDSCAPE Shallow, fertile valley of River Windrush

SUGGESTED MAP OS Explorer 180 Oxford, Witney & Woodstock

START / FINISH Grid reference: SP 323114

DOG FRIENDLINESS Lead essential on road through Crawley and Minster Lovell

PARKING Car park (free) at eastern end of Minster Lovell village, above church and hall

PUBLIC TOILETS None en route

Crawley's industrial heart is announced by its tall mill chimney, which dominates the shallow, verdant valley to the north of Witney. By comparison, a mile or two to the west, old Minster Lovell is the essence of an idealised Cotswold village. Its little houses of grey-brown stone straggle up a narrow street, adorned with impossibly pretty cottage gardens. At the top is a golden stone church, looking down over a silvery meander of the River Windrush. At the bottom is a lovely old pub, the Swan, with the former mill opposite now restored and part of a conference centre.

Two villages appeared on the site in the Domesday Book – Minster Lovell and Little Minster, separated by the river. There's now a newer Minster Lovell to the south-west, an experimental housing and allotment development dating back to the 1840s.

No perfect Cotswold village would be complete without its manor house, of course. And Minster Lovell's is a beauty, although in ruins. The site, in a curve of the river below the church, was picked out by Lord William Lovell, 7th Baron of Tichmarsh, in the 1440s. William's son John extended the new manor house, and signboards among the broken walls show how splendid it must have been, complete with a massive gatehouse.

A Gruesome Tale

William's grandson, Francis, was politically the most successful member of the family, but came to a nasty end. Raised as a Yorkist, he served as Lord Chamberlain to Richard III and fought with him at Bosworth Field in 1485. The King died in the battle and Francis took refuge in Flanders. Two years later he returned to take part in the Lambert Simnel rebellion, which backed an Oxford baker's boy for the throne. On the losing side in a battle at Stoke in 1487, Lovell fled home and was never heard of again. However in 1708, while a new chimney was being built at Minster Lovell Hall, it is said that a locked vault was discovered. In it was the skeleton of the missing Viscount Lovell, sitting with his papers at a table. Exposed to the air, the corpse dissolved into a cloud of dust in an instant. It was assumed that he had hidden here with the help of a servant, who subsequently fell ill and died, leaving unknown the secret of his master's whereabouts. John Buchan made chilling use of the legend in his novel *The Blanket of the Dark* (1931).

A pioneer of modernised agricultural techniques, Thomas Coke was the last resident at the Hall. He left in 1747 for his new Norfolk home, Holkham Hall. The ruins of the Hall are now cared for by English Heritage.

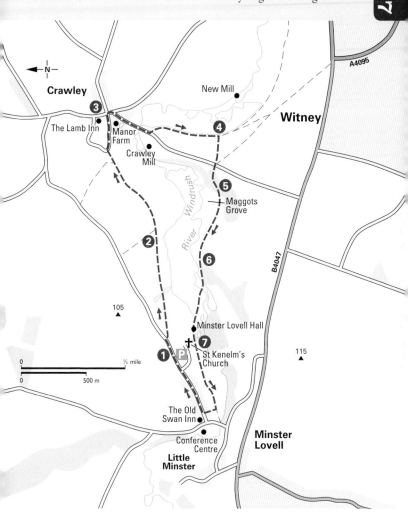

WALK 37 DIRECTIONS

❶ Walk up the lane, signposted 'Crawley'. At the end of the village go through a gate, right, and take the footpath diagonally left across the field, also signposted 'Crawley'. Look right

for a view of the ruins of Minster Lovell Hall and the circular dovecote. Go through a gate near a field gate and continue straight on along the path, with a stone wall to your left. The mill chimney ahead on the horizon belongs to Crawley Mill.

WHAT TO LOOK OUT FOR

Walk through the outline of the ruined Minster Lovell Hall, passing between the spindly tower and the shell of the great hall, to admire the fish ponds. They lie in a tranquil spot below the Church of St Kenelm, shaded by willows and speckled with water lilies. The trout farmed here would have been an important source of food for the Hall, as would the pigeons that lived in the old dovecote.

2 Go through a gate and ahead up a slight incline. Cross two stiles and continue on the path, walking up a green tunnel of a lane. Pass above Crawley Mill. At the road turn right and follow this down into Crawley. At the bottom look left to admire the diminutive village green with its stone cross. The Lamb Inn is on the left.

WHILE YOU'RE THERE

Witney is synonymous with the weaving of fine woollen blankets, which were the garment of choice of the North American Indians. The old firm of Early's, founded in the 17th century, is still going strong, and you can learn more at the Witney Museum. The lively Cogges Manor Farm Museum, a short walk from the town centre, depicts life on a rural farm in Victorian times.

3 Turn right and follow the pavement past Manor Farm, with its huge pond. Cross the humpback bridge over the Windrush – look right for a good view of the old mill house. At the other side of the bridge cross the road and turn left through a gate, signed 'Witney'. Follow the bridleway beside the stream, marked by a line of willows.

4 At the junction of paths by a gate look ahead and left to see New Mill. Turn right through the gate and walk up the field-edge. Pass a gate and cross the road. Go through the gate and straight on to a second gate, and follow the path down through the woods.

5 At the bottom go through a gate and follow the path along the fence. The wildflower meadows of Maggots Grove lie to your right. Continue through four more gates and bear left beside the trees.

6 Go through a gate and enter the woods. At a wooden gate bear right, following the arrows, and cross two footbridges. Continue on the path and cross a bridge over the river. Walk up the meadow towards Minster Lovell Hall. Go through two gates to explore the ruins.

7 Leave by the top entrance and walk through the churchyard. Cross a slab stile, continue along a grassy path with the village up to your right. Cross a footbridge, go through a gate and veer to the right. Go through a gate and then another into Wash Meadow recreation ground. Keep right and go through a gate on to the high street, with The Old Swan pub to your left. Turn right and walk up through the village to the car park.

WHERE TO EAT AND DRINK

The Old Swan Inn lies at the western end of the old village of Minster Lovell, right on the junction with the main road, with The Mill conference centre just opposite. It's a delightful setting, great for teas outside in summer, or a refreshing beer. The Lamb Inn at Crawley also has a restaurant.

Side by Side with the Eastleaches

Two churches, just a stone's throw apart across a narrow stream.

DISTANCE 4 miles (6.4km)　**MINIMUM TIME** 2hrs

ASCENT/GRADIENT 100ft (30m) ▲▲▲　**LEVEL OF DIFFICULTY** +++

PATHS Tracks and lanes, valley paths and woodland, 6 stiles

LANDSCAPE Villages, open wold, narrow valley and streams

SUGGESTED MAP OS Explorer OL45 The Cotswolds

START / FINISH Grid reference: SP 200052

DOG FRIENDLINESS Sheep country – dogs under control at all times

PARKING Village of Eastleach Turville

PUBLIC TOILETS None en route

These two Cotswold villages, sitting cheek by jowl in a secluded valley, carry an air of quiet perfection. And yet Eastleach Turville and Eastleach Martin are quite distinctive, and each has a parish church (though one is now redundant). St Andrews in Eastleach Turville faces St Michael and St Martin's across the narrow River Leach. Their origins lie in the development of the parish system from the earliest days of the Anglo-Saxon Church.

The Anglo-Saxon Kingdoms

The English parish has its origins in the shifting rivalries of Saxon England; for the one thing that united the various Saxon kingdoms was the Church. The first 'parishes' were really the Anglo-Saxon kingdoms. Christianity, the new power in the land, not only saved souls but also secured alliances. The Pope's aim was to invest more bishops to act as pastors and proselytisers, but at the same time their appointments were useful politically, helping to smooth the way as larger kingdoms absorbed their smaller neighbours. The number of appointments would also depend on local factors. Wessex, for example, was divided into shires and so a bishop was appointed for each one. Later the Normans appointed Archdeacons, whose job was to ensure that church buildings were maintained for worship. Over the centuries the assorted conventions and appointments that had accumulated through usage coalesced into a hierarchical English Church. For a long time, however, control was not tight. Missionaries, for example, would occasionally land from Ireland and found their own churches, quite independently of local potentates. Rulers and local landholders were certainly influential in the development of the parish system, but many parishes also derived from the gradual disintegration of the local 'minster', a central church on consecrated ground which controlled a group of client chapels. As population and congregations grew, the chapels themselves became new parish churches, with rights equal to those of the minster. This included the right to bury the dead in their own graveyard and administration of births and marriages.

THE EASTLEACHES

Tithe Payments

With the passage of time and the establishment of a single English kingdom, the idea of a parish had diminished geographically to something akin to its modern size. By the 10th century the parish had become the accepted framework for the enforcement of the payment of tithes, the medieval equivalent of an income tax. By the 12th century much of the modern diocesan map of England was established. So in the Eastleaches, all these developments come together and you find two parish churches virtually side by side. With politics, power and bureaucracy all playing a part, it's likely that the pastoral needs of the community were quite a long way down the list of factors which led to their creation.

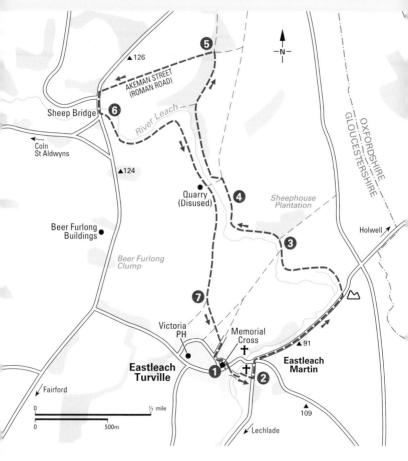

WALK 38 DIRECTIONS

1 From the memorial cross in Eastleach Turville walk along the road with the river on your right. After a few paces locate a path on your right to cross the clapper bridge and follow the path into the churchyard of Eastleach Martin.

Pass to the right of the church and emerge at a road.

2 Turn left and then turn right at a junction, finally taking the lower road in the direction of Holwell. Walk on for perhaps 600yds (549m) to where the road begins to rise steeply. Turn left here, pass through a gate into a field, and follow an obvious grassy track at the base of a slope for 0.5 mile (800m).

❸ This will bring you to a gate at the corner of Sheephouse Plantation. Go through the gate and follow the woods to your right. Continue to a gate at a field – do not go through this but continue forward with the field to your right. Soon you will reach a small area of scrubby trees, turn right here over a stile into a field and turn left.

> ### WHAT TO LOOK OUT FOR
> The little clapper bridge linking the two parishes is known locally as Keble's Bridge, after a family who were eminent in the area. John Keble, for whom Keble College in Oxford is named, was nominal curate for the two parishes in the 19th century. In the middle part of the walk the straight track to a road is part of Akeman Street, the Roman road that linked Cirencester with St Albans.

❹ Continue, passing through gates, until you come to a gated bridge on your left. Do not cross this but continue forward towards a gate at the edge of woodland. Go through and follow a woodland path until you emerge at a clearing. Walk to the other side to re-enter woodland and continue to a track.

❺ Turn left here and follow the track out of the woods and across fields until you come to a road. Turn left here, cross Sheep Bridge and, just before a turning to the right, go left into a field.

❻ Bear right along the valley bottom, then left and right again. This will bring you to a gate. Go

> ### WHERE TO EAT AND DRINK
> Eastleach Turville has a lovely little pub, the Victoria, in the western part of the village. Nearby Southrop, to the south, also has The Swan, a creeper-clad old pub with real fires in winter and a wide choice of food. In Coln St Alwyns, to the west, you'll find The New Inn, everybody's idea of a classic Cotswold pub and serving excellent food.

through it, on to a track, and soon pass the gated bridge again. Follow the wall on your right as it curves up to a gate and then stay on the same line through gates until you reach a gate into the last field bordering Eastleach Turville.

❼ Turn half left across this field, heading for a gate just to the right of a prominent horse chestnut tree. Join the lane here, and keep left at the fork to return to your car at the start.

> ### WHILE YOU'RE THERE
> There are two places near by worth visiting while you are in the area. To the south is Lechlade, Gloucestershire's only settlement on the River Thames. There is a handsome market square, an idyllic riverside and several fascinating old streets to wander through. To the west is Fairford, a handsome village noted for its fine church containing one of the only sets of medieval stained glass in the country.

WALK 39

Around the Lakes of the Cotswold Water Park

Through an evolving landscape in the southern Cotswolds

DISTANCE 5 miles (8km)   MINIMUM TIME 2hrs 30min

ASCENT/GRADIENT Negligible ▲▲▲   LEVEL OF DIFFICULTY ✦✦✦

PATHS Track, tow path and lanes

LANDSCAPE Dead flat – lakes, light woodland, canal and village

SUGGESTED MAP OS Explorer 169 Cirencester & Swindon

START / FINISH Grid reference: SU 048974

DOG FRIENDLINESS Good but be aware of a lot of waterfowl around lakes

PARKING Silver Street, South Cerney

PUBLIC TOILETS None en route

By their very nature, ancient landscapes and historic architecture evolve very slowly, changing little from one century to another. Can they resist the demands of a brasher era? In the Cotswolds the answer to this question is essentially 'yes'. Here building restrictions are strict – even, sometimes, draconian. The result, however, is a significant area of largely unspoilt English countryside; sometimes, thoughtful development has even enhanced an otherwise lacklustre skyline. The Cotswold Water Park, located in and around old gravel pits, is an example of this.

Recreational Gravel

Gravel has been worked in the upper Thames Valley, where the water table is close to the surface, since the 1920s. The removal of gravel leads to the creation of lakes and in the areas around South Cerney and between Fairford and Lechlade there are now some 4,000 acres (1,620ha) of water, in 133 lakes. They provide an important wetland habitat for a variety of wildlife. Most of these lakes have been turned over to recreational use of one sort or another, being a perfect place for game and coarse fishing, board sailing, walking, boating of various kinds, riding and sundry other leisure activities. Interestingly, this has been what is now called a private/ public enterprise. The landscaping has not just been a case of letting nature take over where the gravel excavators left off. The crane-grabs that were used for excavation in the 1960s, for example, left the gravel pits with vertical sides and therefore with deep water right up to the shoreline. As it happens, some forms of aquatic life flourish under these conditions, but in other lakes the shoreline has been graded to create a gentler slope, to harmonise better with the flat landscape in this part of the Cotswolds and to suit the needs of swimmers and children. In the same way, trees have been planted and hills have been constructed to offer shelter and visual relief. Old brick railway bridges have been preserved. Finally, a style of waterside architecture has been developed to attract people to live here. The landscape continues to evolve, just as the surrounding countryside has done for centuries.

South Cerney and Cerney Wick

The walk begins in South Cerney, by the River Churn, only 4 miles (6.4km) from the source of the Thames. Look inside the Norman church for the carving on the 12th-century rood. Later the walk takes you through Cerney Wick, a small village on the other side of the gravel workings. The highlight here is an 18th-century roundhouse, used once by canal workers.

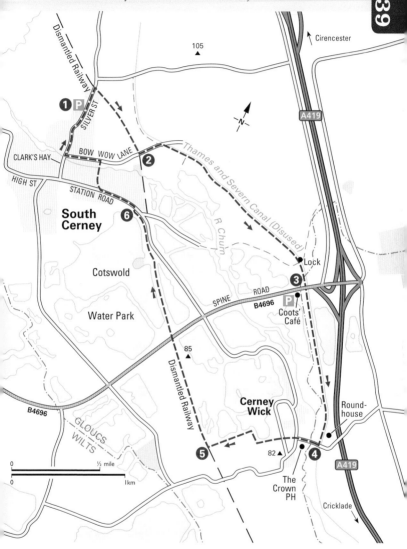

WALK 39 DIRECTIONS

❶ From Silver Street walk north out of the village. Just before the turning to Driffield and Cricklade, turn right on to National Cycle Route 45. Stay on this obvious path for 800yds (732m), to reach a brick bridge across the path. Turn right here up a flight of steps to reach a narrow road.

❷ Turn left and walk along here for 200yds (183m) until you come

SOUTH CERNEY

to footpaths to the right and left. Turn right along a farm track, following a signpost for Cerney Wick. Almost immediately the shallow, overgrown remains of the Thames and Severn Canal appear to your left. When the track veers right into a farm, walk ahead over a stile to follow a path beneath the trees – the old canal tow path. Keep ahead through kissing gates as you pass the partly restored Wildmoorway Lower Lock, just before the Spine Road Bridge.

❸ Continue under the bridge and past Coots' Café until the path forks at an information panel. Here you have two choices: either continue on the tow path or take the path that skirts the lakes. If you take the lakeside path, you will eventually be able to rejoin the tow path by going left at a bridge after 600yds (549m). Continue until, after just under 0.5 mile (800m), you pass an old canal roundhouse across the canal to the left and, soon after, reach a lane at Cerney Wick.

❹ Turn right here and walk to the junction at the end of the road, beside The Crown pub. Cross to a stile and enter a field. Walk straight ahead and come to another stile. Cross this aiming to the left of a cottage. Cross the lane, go through a kissing gate

and enter a field. Walk ahead and follow the path as it guides you through a kissing gate and across a stile on to the grass by a lake. Walk around the lake, going right and then left. In the corner in front of you, cross into a field, then walk ahead towards trees and cross a stile to a track.

❺ Turn right, rejoining the old railway line and follow it all the way to the Spine Road. Cross with care, and continue along National Cycle Route 45. Stay on this all the way to another road and follow a path that runs to its left.

❻ Where the path ends at the beginning of South Cerney, continue along Station Road for 400yds (440m). A few paces past The Lennards on your right, turn right up the signposted footpath that takes you across a bridge and brings you to a lane called Bow Wow. Turn left here between streams and return to Silver Street and the start of the route.

Right: Cotswold Water Park

Larks Above Down Ampney

*A route based on the birthplace of one of
Britain's best-known composers.*

DISTANCE 10 miles (16.1km)   **MINIMUM TIME** 4hrs

ASCENT/GRADIENT 100ft (30m) ▲▲▲   **LEVEL OF DIFFICULTY** +++

PATHS Fields, lanes, tracks, 9 stiles

LANDSCAPE Generally level fields and villages in all directions

SUGGESTED MAP OS Explorer 169 Cirencester & Swindon

START / FINISH Grid reference: SU 099965

DOG FRIENDLINESS On lead near livestock but plenty of stretches without

PARKING Down Ampney village

PUBLIC TOILETS None en route

Ralph Vaughan Williams is considered by many to be England's greatest composer. He was born in 1872 in Down Ampney, where his father was vicar, spending the first three years of his life in the Old Vicarage. He studied music in London at the Royal College of Music with Parry, Stanford and Wood, who were the leading British musicians of the day. Then he studied in Berlin with Bruch and later in Paris with Ravel. This experience gave him the confidence to tackle large-scale works, many of which were based on English folk songs, which he had begun to collect in 1903. But Vaughan Williams was also interested in early English liturgical music, the result of which was his *Fantasia on a Theme by Thomas Tallis* (1910) for strings, which combines the English lyrical, pastoral tradition with the stricter demands of early formal composition.

Famous Works

Vaughan Williams went on to compose several symphonies, as well as a ballet based on the ideas of William Blake, and an opera based on *The Pilgrim's Progress* by John Bunyan. There were several sacred works, too, including a Mass and the Revelation oratorio. He also composed the score for the film *Scott of the Antarctic* (1948). One of his best-known hymn tunes is *Down Ampney* (1906), named in tribute to his birthplace. For many of us, however, Vaughan Williams is associated with two pieces in particular. The first is his version of *Greensleeves* (1928), the song said to have been originally composed by Henry VIII; and the second is *The Lark Ascending* (1914), the soaring work for violin and orchestra.

There are four Ampneys altogether. Down Ampney church is the finest and definitely worth a visit. It's crowned by a 14th-century spire and contains several interesting effigies. Adjacent to the church is Down Ampney House, a 15th-century manor house that was later redesigned by Sir John Soane. The prettiest of the villages is Ampney Crucis, which takes its name from the 14th-century cross in the churchyard. The head of the cross was only rediscovered in 1854, having been secreted in the church, probably to protect it from puritan zealots in the 16th or 17th century.

Buscot to Kelmscott

On the Thames Path to the home of William Morris.

DISTANCE 4.75 miles (7.7km) **MINIMUM TIME** 2hrs

ASCENT/GRADIENT 82ft (25m) ▲▲▲ **LEVEL OF DIFFICULTY** +++

PATHS Riverside paths, fields, village lanes, 6 stiles

LANDSCAPE Open, flat lands of the Thames floodplain

SUGGESTED MAP OS Explorer 170 Abingdon, Wantage & Vale of White Horse

START / FINISH Grid reference: SU 231976

DOG FRIENDLINESS On lead around weir, not permitted in Manor gardens

PARKING National Trust car park (free) in Buscot, signed 'Buscot Weir'

PUBLIC TOILETS Buscot, behind phone box

The village of Kelmscott is famous for its connections with the founder of the Arts and Crafts Movement, William Morris (1834–96). Today he is best remembered for his furnishing designs, rich with flowers, leaves and birds, still popular on fabric and wallpaper.

Champion of Fine Craftsmanship

Throughout his life, working with great Pre-Raphaelite artists such as Edward Burne-Jones and Dante Gabriel Rossetti, Morris dedicated himself to a movement against what he saw as the vulgar tastes of his day, with its sentimentality, clutter and gewgaws. He put a new value on craftsmanship, studying and experimenting with the techniques of ages past, and so developing a style of apparent simplicity combined with functionality. He took it upon himself to educate as well as create, with pronouncements such as 'Have nothing in your houses that you do not know to be useful, or believe to be beautiful' emphasising the place of good design in everyday life. His philosophy of design became hugely influential.

Morris looked to the medieval artists and architects for his inspiration – a favourite outing for visitors to Kelmscott was to the magnificent Great Barn, a medieval stone-built tithe barn at nearby Great Coxwell (now cared for by the National Trust), to admire the intricacies and craftsmanship of its soaring timber roof.

Manor and Village

Kelmscott Manor itself dates from 1570 and became Morris's country home in 1871. It's a mellow old place, built of the local grey limestone, with mullioned windows and high pointed gables topped by ball finials. (The image is familiar from the woodcut designed for the Kelmscott Press, which he founded in 1890.) Morris loved the manor for its integrity and austerity, and for the harmony of the house in its setting, almost as if 'it had grown up out of the soil'. Now owned by the Society of Antiquaries of London, the house is open to the public on Wednesdays and some Saturdays through the summer, and contains many examples of Morris's work.

BUSCOT

William Morris's influence on the area continued even after his death. As a memorial to the great man, several structures were designed to his principles and built in Kelmscott village, notably Memorial Cottages and next-door Manor Cottages. On a wider scale, Morris's work did much for the emergence of a Cotswold identity in the 1920s, with his appreciation and publicising of the vernacular architecture.

Morris is buried with his wife and daughters in the churchyard at Kelmscott, under a modest tombstone.

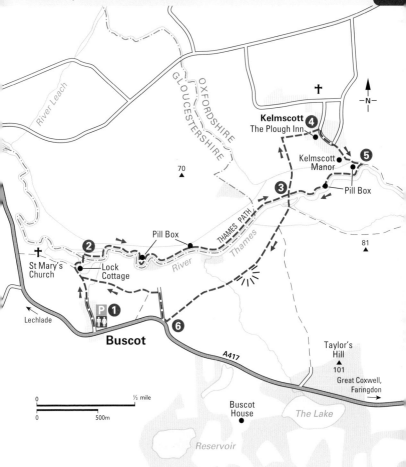

WALK 41 DIRECTIONS

1 Turn left and walk back into Buscot to admire the arcaded pump. Retrace your steps and continue ahead on the road, signed to the weir. Follow the road past the Village Field. Keep right down a path to pass Lock Cottage. Follow the footpath over a weir. Then bear left and cross the lock gate.

2 Turn right immediately, pass the lock, go through a gate and follow the path beside the river. Soon bear left through a gate and cross a bridge, with a view left to the main weir. Turn right and follow the Thames Path beside the meandering river. Go through two gates, and continue past two wartime pill boxes and a gate. Go through a pair of gates. The roofs of Kelmscott appear ahead. Go through a gate and continue towards the bridge, passing through some trees.

❸ Pass the bridge, go through a gate and turn left through a squeeze stile up the field. At the far side cross a stile and two footbridges. Bear left and ahead up the hedge (yellow waymarker). At the end turn right along the path, which may be overgrown. Follow this into Kelmscott village.

WHAT TO LOOK OUT FOR

Look out for the charming relief carving of William Morris, set in the wall of the pair of Memorial Cottages at first floor height, between the windows. The great man is shown sitting under a tree, listening to the birds, with the old wool barn and summer house of the manor in the background (shown right).

❹ Turn right to pass The Plough Inn. Bear left along the road, passing Memorial Cottages and Manor Cottages. Keep right to reach Kelmscott Manor. Maintain your direction ahead down the track and turn right just before you get to the river.

❺ Cross a bridge and go through a gate to join the Thames Path National Trail. Go through a gateway and continue, passing another old wartime pill box on your right. Go through the gate by the footbridge and turn left over the bridge. Bear left and right over another bridge. Cross a stile and walk up the track. Soon this crosses a ditch; now head diagonally right across the field. At the corner cross a stile and footbridge by the fingerpost and turn right. Keep straight on up the edge of the field, with views of Buscot House, left. Follow the track downhill, and bend right, then turn left over a footbridge. Continue on the path diagonally right across the next two fields.

WHERE TO EAT AND DRINK

The friendly Plough Inn at Kelmscott is a lovely old pub, with a flagstone floor and beautifully refurbished oak panelling. There's a beer garden at the front and a restaurant at the rear, with a lunch menu that changes according to the season – from mushrooms on toast to more exotic pasta dishes, as well as sandwiches. Dogs are welcome at the bar.

❻ Go through a gate by the road and turn right up a drive. Look out for a yellow waymarker and take the footpath off to the left. Soon cross a stile and veer left along the edge of the field. Cross a stile and a footbridge at the other end, walk across the Village Field and turn left to retrace your route back to your car at the start of the walk in Buscot.

WHILE YOU'RE THERE

St Mary's Church at Buscot has some good examples of stained glass from the firm of Morris and Co, founded by William Morris in 1861. The colours are rich, the foliage sumptuous in its detail. The window above the altar is by Burne-Jones. Look, too, for the unusual painted pulpit and two touching marble memorials to the first and second wives of Edward Loveden Loveden Esq, who died within four years of each other.

The Infant Thames at Cricklade

*An easy ramble across water-meadows beside the
Thames and disused canals.*

> **DISTANCE** 5.5 miles (8.8km)   **MINIMUM TIME** 2hrs 30min
>
> **ASCENT/GRADIENT** Negligible ▲▲▲   **LEVEL OF DIFFICULTY** ✦✦✦
>
> **PATHS** Field paths and bridle paths, disused railway, town streets, 6 stiles
>
> **LANDSCAPE** Flat river valley
>
> **SUGGESTED MAP** OS Explorer 169 Cirencester & Swindon
>
> **START / FINISH** Grid reference: SU 100934
>
> **DOG FRIENDLINESS** Dogs can be off lead along old railway line
>
> **PARKING** Cricklade Town Hall car park (free)
>
> **PUBLIC TOILETS** Cricklade High Street

The River Thames begins life in a peaceful Gloucestershire field near Cirencester. Before long it graduates to a sizeable stream, also known as the Isis at this point, on its way to the Cotswold Water Park, a vast network of lakes and pools, before reaching Cricklade, Wiltshire's northernmost town and the only one situated on the river.

Although merely a meandering willow-fringed stream as it passes through the town, research in the 19th century revealed that the river at Cricklade had been navigable by large barges during the 17th and 18th centuries. In 1607 the Burcot Commission was established for the purpose of improving the Thames as a navigable waterway from Clifton Hampden to Cricklade. With the completion of the Thames and Severn Canal in 1789 river traffic was transferred to the canal and the upper reaches of the Thames gradually became overgrown.

Cricklade – Roman Military Post

Cricklade's advantageous position at the junction of four ancient roads may well be why it was established as the head of the navigable Thames. However, Cricklade's importance as a settlement began in Roman times when it was a significant military post on Ermine Street, the Roman road linking Cirencester and Silchester. Evidence of Roman occupation has been found in and around the town, with villas to the north and south-east. The later fortified Saxon town was built as a defence against the Danes and had its own mint. Today, the High Street has worthy buildings from the 17th and 18th centuries and two contrasting parish churches. You should not miss St Sampson's, characterised by its cathedral-like turreted tower that rises high above the town and dominates the surrounding water-meadows.

Abandoned Communication Lines

This walk follows the River Thames north, away from Cricklade, via the Thames Path. Beyond North Meadow, your route passes beside a shallow ditch that was once the North Wilts Canal, which opened in 1819 and ran the 9 miles (14.5km) between Swindon and Latton, linking the Wilts

CRICKLADE

and Berks Canal with the Thames and Severn Canal. Soon you will follow the old tow path beside the muddy, weed-clogged ditch that was once the Thames and Severn Canal, opened in 1789 to link the River Severn with the Thames at Lechlade. The canal closed to all traffic in 1927, and was finally abandoned in 1933. Later the walk heads south along a disused railway line, part of the Midland and South West Railway which was closed to passengers in 1961. Although a pleasing reminder of the railway era, the ever-present drone of traffic from the A419 across the water-meadows keeps the mind firmly in the 21st century.

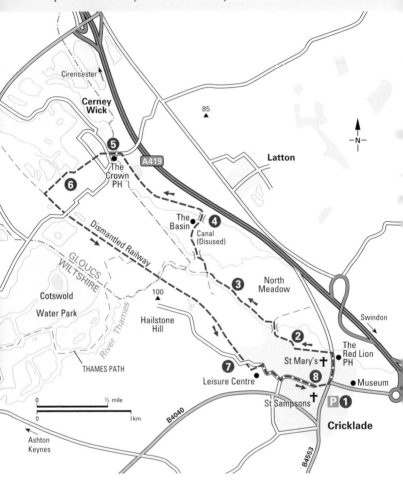

WALK 42 DIRECTIONS

❶ Turn right out of the car park, keep ahead at the roundabout and walk along the High Street. Pass St Mary's Church, then turn left along North Wall before the river bridge. Shortly, bear right to a gate and join the Thames Path.

Continue your route along the field-edge to houses.

❷ Go through the kissing gate on your right and bear left across the field to a gate. Follow the fenced footpath, cross a plank bridge and pass through the gate immediately on your right-hand side. Cross the

and bear off left (yellow arrow) into trees.

6 Cross a footbridge and proceed ahead along the field edge to a stile. Turn left along the old railway, signed 'Cricklade'. Cross the River Thames in a mile (1.6km) and keep to the path along the former trackbed to reach a bridge.

river bridge and turn left through a gate. Walk beside the infant River Thames, crossing two gates to enter North Meadow.

3 Continue to cross a stile by a bridge. Go through the gate immediately right and keep straight ahead, ignoring the Thames Path, left. Follow the path beside the disused canal. Cross a footbridge and a stile then, at a fence, bear right to cross a footbridge close to a house named The Basin. Bear right along the drive.

4 Cross a bridge and turn left through the gateway. Shortly, bear right to join the path along the left side of the old canal. Keep to the path for 0.5 mile (800m) to the road. Turn left into Cerney Wick to reach a T-junction.

5 Cross the stone stile opposite and keep ahead through the paddock to a stone stile and lane. Cross the lane and go through the gate opposite, continuing ahead to a kissing gate and stile. Follow the path ahead. Bear right, then left

7 Follow the gravel path to the Leisure Centre. Bear left on to the road, following it right, then turn left opposite the entrance to the Leisure Centre car park. Turn right, then next left and follow the road to the church.

8 Walk beside the barrier and turn right in front of The Gatehouse into the churchyard. Bear left to the main gates and follow the lane to a T-junction. Turn right to make your way back to the car park.

Sherston and Easton Grey's Cotswold Fringe

The infant Bristol Avon links attractive stone villages on this pastoral ramble on the south-eastern fringes of the Cotswolds

---

DISTANCE 6.5 miles (10.4km)   **MINIMUM TIME** 3hrs

ASCENT/GRADIENT 131ft (40m) ▲▲▲   **LEVEL OF DIFFICULTY** +++

PATHS Field and parkland paths, tracks, metalled lanes, 13 stiles

LANDSCAPE River valley and gently rolling farmland

SUGGESTED MAP OS Explorer 168 Stroud, Tetbury & Malmesbury

START / FINISH Grid reference: ST 853858

DOG FRIENDLINESS Dogs can be off lead along Fosse Way

PARKING Sherston High Street; plenty of roadside parking

PUBLIC TOILETS None en route

The Bristol Avon rises in the foothills of the Cotswolds in the north-west corner of Wiltshire and is little more than a wide and shallow stream as it flows through the gently rolling pastoral countryside west of Malmesbury. Despite its size, this peaceful river enhances all the charming little stone villages in this unspoilt and somewhat forgotten area of north Wiltshire, which is typically Cotswold in appearance and character. In fact, 18 villages between Colerne and Malmesbury are officially part of the Cotswold Area of Outstanding Natural Beauty. Of these, Sherston must rank among the most attractive, with its wide High Street, doubtless once used as a market, lined with some interesting 17th- and 18th-century buildings. Sherston was a borough by the 15th century and prospered as a result of the flourishing wool trade at the time. It still has the feel of a market town, with narrow back streets and alleys, and continues to be a thriving community despite becoming a dormitory village.

Legend of a Local Hero

It has been suggested that Sherston is Sceorstan, as chronicled by Henry of Huntingdon, where in 1016 Edmund Ironside won a battle against the Danes who were led by King Canute. The early legend of John Rattlebone, a local yeoman promised land by Ironside in return for service against the Danes is deep rooted. Sadly, this brave knight was terribly wounded in battle and although he staunched his bleeding with a stone tile and continued fighting, he reputedly died as Canute's army withdrew. Other traditions say Rattlebone survived to claim his reward.

In the 17th century, the antiquary John Aubrey recorded the following local rhyme: 'Fight well, Rattlebone, Thou shalt have Sherston, What shall I with Sherston do, Without I have all belongs thereto? Thou shalt have Wych and Wellesley, Easton Town and Pinkeney.' Later traditions tell us that the small stone effigy on the south side of the porch outside the parish church is that of Rattlebone, and that an ancient timber chest in the church, marked with the initials R B, is supposed to be where Rattlebone kept his armour. Whatever the truth is, the Rattlebone Inn opposite the church keeps his name alive.

Easton Grey – Pure Cotswold Charm

Peaceful parkland and riverside paths lead you downstream to picturesque Easton Grey. Set around a 16th-century stone bridge and climbing a short, curving street is an intimate huddle of ancient stone houses, with mullioned windows, steep, lichen-covered roofs and colourful, flower-filled gardens that touch the river bank. Set back on a rise above the river is Easton Grey House, a handsome 18th-century manor house with a classical façade and portico, surrounded by elegant gardens and lovely valley views. It was the summer retreat of Herbert Asquith, 1st Earl of Oxford, when he was Prime Minister between 1908 and 1916.

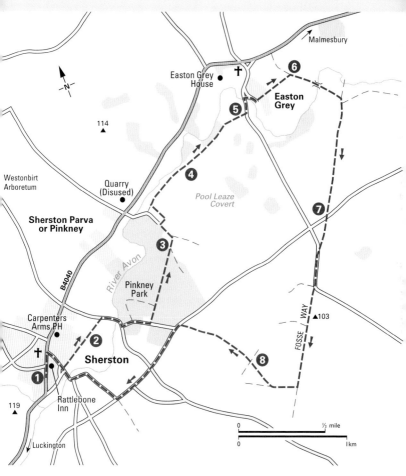

WALK 43 DIRECTIONS

❶ On Sherton's High Street, walk towards the village stores, pass the Rattlebone Inn and turn right into Noble Street. Pass Grove Road and take the footpath left up a flight of steps. Cross a

cul-de-sac and follow the metalled footpath to a gate. Continue at the rear of houses to a further gate.

❷ Bear diagonally right across a field to a stile, followed by a gate leading out to a lane. Turn right, cross the river and turn

SHERSTON

left, signed 'Foxley'. At the end of woodland on your left, take the footpath left through a gate. Follow the track across Pinkney Park to a gate.

3 Keep ahead, bearing left beside the wall to a gate. Immediately beyond it turn right for several paces, then left through a gate. Follow the path round the edge of a field to a stile. Cross it, then go immediately right over the adjacent stile. Aim for the left-hand corner of the field to the next stile. Keep alongside the fence to the next stile and bear right to a gate.

4 Go diagonally across the field with Easton Grey House visible in the distance. Cross two stiles with a footbridge in between and head downhill to a gate and lane.

5 Turn left into Easton Grey. Cross the river bridge, turn right uphill to take the footpath ahead on reaching entrance gates on your right. Cross a gravelled area, go through a gate and keep ahead to a stile. Maintain direction across the next field and gently descend to follow a track into the next field.

6 Turn right along the field-edge and bear off right in the corner, downhill through scrub to a footbridge. Keep ahead beside a ruin to a gate. Cross a stile and continue to a further stile and gate. Follow the track downhill to a stile and turn right along a track (Fosse Way). Continue for just over 0.5 mile (around 900m) to a road.

7 Cross straight over and keep to the byway to another road. Bear left and keep ahead where the lane veers sharp left. Follow this rutted track for 0.5 mile (800m), then cross the arrowed stile on your right. Head across the field to a stile and continue ahead beside a hedge to a gate. Turn right then immediately left, skirt a paddock and join a track.

8 Cross a racehorse gallop to a gate. Walk through scrub to another gate and keep to the track ahead to a road. Turn left and continue to a crossroads. Proceed straight on to the next junction and keep ahead, following the lane all the way back into Sherston.

Castle Combe and By Brook

Through the wooded By Brook Valley from a famous picture-book village.

DISTANCE 5.75 miles (9.2km)   **MINIMUM TIME** 2hrs 30min

ASCENT/GRADIENT 515ft (157m) ▲▲▲   **LEVEL OF DIFFICULTY** ✦✦✦

PATHS Field and woodland paths and tracks, metalled lanes, 10 stiles

LANDSCAPE Wooded river valley and village streets

SUGGESTED MAP OS Explorer 156 Chippenham & Bradford-on-Avon

START / FINISH Grid reference: ST 845776

DOG FRIENDLINESS Keep under control across pasture and golf course

PARKING Free car park just off B4039 at Upper Castle Combe

PUBLIC TOILETS Castle Combe

Since being voted 'the prettiest village in England' in 1962, there have been more visitors to Castle Combe, more photographs taken of it and more words written about it than any other village in the county. Nestling deep in a steam-threaded combe, just a mile (1.6km), and a world away, from the M4, it certainly has all the elements to make it a tourist's dream. You'll find 15th-century Cotswold stone cottages with steep gabled roofs surrounding a turreted church and stone-canopied market cross, a medieval manor house, a fast-flowing steam in the main street leading to an ancient packhorse bridge and a perfectly picturesque river.

Yet, as preservation is taken so seriously here, a palpable atmosphere of unreality surrounds this tiny 'toytown', where television aerials don't exist, gardens are immaculately kept, and the inevitable commercialism is carefully concealed. Behind this present-day façade, however, exists a fascinating history that's well worth exploring, and the timeless valleys and tumbling wooded hillsides that surround the village are favourite Wiltshire walking destinations. If you don't like crowds and really want to enjoy Castle Combe, undertake this walk on a winter weekday.

'Castlecombe' Cloth

The castle, which gave the village its name, began life as a Roman fort and was used by the Saxons before becoming a Norman castle in 1135 and the home of the de Dunstanville family. In the 13th and 14th centuries the village established itself as an important weaving centre as Sir John Fastolf, the lord of the manor, erected fulling mills along the By Brook and 50 cottages for his workers. With the growth of the cloth trade in Wiltshire, Castle Combe prospered greatly, becoming more like a town with a weekly market and an annual fair.

The greatest tribute to the wealth of the weaving industry is reflected in St Andrew's Church which was enlarged during the 15th century. Its impressive Perpendicular tower was built in 1436. For centuries the villages produced a red and white cloth known as Castlecombe. Cloth manufacture began to decline in the early 18th century when the diminutive By Brook

CASTLE COMBE

was unable to power the larger machinery being introduced. People moved to the larger towns and Castle Combe became depopulated and returned to an agricultural existence. An annual fair, centred around the Market Cross, continued until 1904, and Castle Combe remained an 'estate' village until 1947 when the whole village was sold at auction.

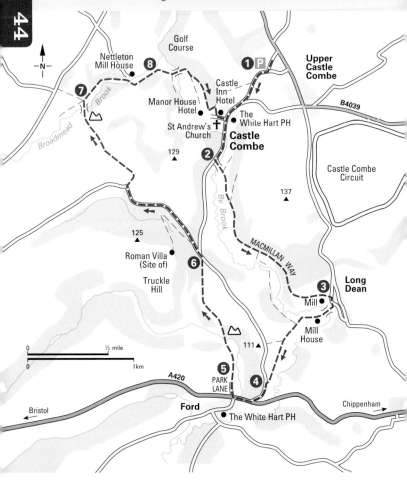

WALK 44 DIRECTIONS

❶ Leave the car park via the steps and turn right. At the T-junction, turn right and follow the lane into Castle Combe. Keep left at the Market Cross, cross the By Brook and continue along the road to take the path, signed 'Long Dean', across the second bridge on your left.

❷ Pass through a gate and follow the path uphill and then beside the right-hand fence above the valley (Macmillan Way). Beyond an open area, gently ascend through woodland to a stone stile and gate. Cross a further stile and descend into the hamlet of Long Dean.

❸ Pass the mill and, where the lane bears left, follow the track right to cross the river bridge. At a mill house, keep right and follow the sunken bridleway uphill to a gate. Shortly enter sloping pasture

CASTLE COMBE

and follow the defined path around the top edge, bearing left to reach a stile and lane.

❹ Turn left and descend to the A420 at Ford. Turn right along the pavement and shortly turn right again into Park Lane. (If you want to visit The White Hart in Ford village, take the road ahead on your left, signed 'Colerne'.) Climb the gravel track and take the footpath left through a squeeze stile.

❺ Keep right through pasture and continue through trees to a water-meadow in the valley bottom. Turn left, cross a stile and a stream and steeply ascend the grassy slope ahead of you, bearing left beyond some trees towards a waymarker post. Follow the footpath along the top of the field to a stile and gate, then walk through the woodland to a gate and the road.

❻ Turn left, then immediately left again, signed 'North Wraxall'. Keep to the road for 0.5 mile (800m) and take the arrowed bridleway, right. Follow the track then, just before a gate, keep right downhill on a sunken path to come to a footbridge over Broadmead Brook.

❼ In 20yds (18m), climb the stile on your right and follow the footpath close to the river. Cross a stile and soon pass beside Nettleton Mill House, bearing right to a hidden gate. Walk beside the stream, cross a stile and you will soon reach the golf course.

❽ Turn right along the metalled track, cross the bridge and turn immediately right again. At a gate, follow the path left below the golf course fairway. Walk beside a wall to reach a stile on your right. Drop down to a metalled drive and keep ahead back into Castle Combe. Turn left at the Market Cross and retrace your steps.

WHILE YOU'RE THERE
Linger by the bridge over the By Brook and recall, if you've seen it, the 1966 film *Dr Doolittle*. Although miles from the coast, a jetty was built on the banks in front of the 17th-century cottages here to create a fishing harbour, complete with seven boats and plastic cobbles. Local people became 'extras' at £2 10s per day, with meals, alcohol and clothes all thrown in.

WHAT TO LOOK OUT FOR
St Andrew's Church, in Castle Combe, is worth closer inspection. On the parapet, note the 50 stone heads and the carving of a shuttle and scissors, the mark of the cloth industry put there by merchants who built the church. Inside, don't miss the rare faceless clock made by a local blacksmith in 1380, and the 13th-century tomb of Sir Walter de Dunstanville. Along the By Brook, note the former fulling mills and weavers' cottages at the remote and unspoilt hamlet of Long Dean.

Brunel's Great Tunnel Through Box Hill

*A hilly walk around Box Hill, famous for its stone
and Brunel's greatest engineering achievement.*

DISTANCE 3.25 miles (5.3km) **MINIMUM TIME** 1hr 45min

ASCENT/GRADIENT 508ft (155m) ▲▲▲ **LEVEL OF DIFFICULTY** ✦✦✦

PATHS Field and woodland paths, bridleways, lanes, 16 stiles

LANDSCAPE River valley and wooded hillsides

SUGGESTED MAP OS Explorer 156 Chippenham & Bradford-on-Avon

START / FINISH Grid reference: ST 824686

DOG FRIENDLINESS Can be off lead on Box Hill Common and in woodland

PARKING Village car park near Selwyn Hall

PUBLIC TOILETS Opposite Queens Head in Box

B ox is a large straggling village that sits astride the busy A4 in hilly country halfway between Bath and Chippenham. Although stone has been quarried here since the 9th century, Box really found fame during the 18th century when the local stone was used for Bath's magnificent buildings. The construction of Box Tunnel uncovered immense deposits of good stone and by 1900 Box stone quarries were among the most productive in the world. Little trace can be seen above ground today, except for some fine stone-built houses in the village and a few reminders on Box Hill.

Appointed Engineer

In 1833, the newly created Great Western Railway appointed Isambard Kingdom Brunel (1806–59) as engineer. His task was to build a railway covering the 118 miles (190km) from London to Bristol. The problems and projects he encountered on the way would help to make him the most famous engineer of the Victorian age. After a relatively straightforward and level start through the Home Counties, he came to the hilly Cotswolds.

Brunel's Famous Tunnel

The solution at Box would be a tunnel, and at nearly 2 miles (3.2km) long and with a gradient of 1:100 it would be the longest and steepest in the world at the time. It would also be very wide. Already controversial, Brunel ignored the gauge of other companies, preferring the 7ft (2.1m) used by tramways and roads (and, it was believed, Roman chariots). He also made the tunnel dead straight, and, never one to 'hide his light', the alignment was calculated so the dawn sun would shine through on his birthday on 9th April. Unfortunately he did not allow for atmospheric refraction and was two days out!

Passage to Narnia?

All was on a grand scale: a ton of gunpowder and candles were used every week, 3 million bricks were fired to line the soft Cotswold limestone and 100 navvies lost their lives working on the tunnel. After 2.5 years the way was open, and although Brunel would ultimately lose the battle of the gauges, his magnificent line meant that Bristol was then a mere two hours from the capital. Although artificial, like many large dark holes, the tunnel has collected its fair share of mystery with tales of noises, people under the hill and trains entering the tunnel, never to re-emerge. But as is often the case, the explanations are rather more mundane. To test excavation conditions, Brunel dug a small trial section alongside what is now the eastern entrance and the military commandeered this section during World War Two as a safe and fairly secret store for ammunition, records and top brass. Sadly it is not a passage to Narnia!

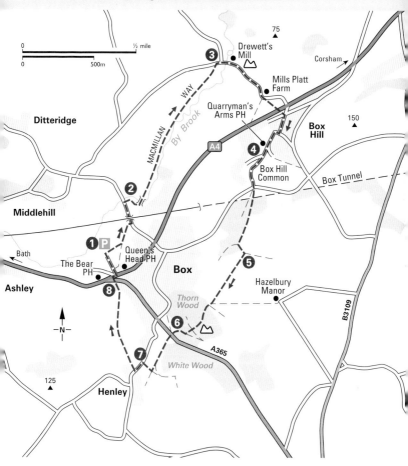

WALK 45 DIRECTIONS

❶ Facing the recreation ground, walk to the left-hand side of the football pitch to join a track in the corner close to the railway line. When you reach the lane, turn left, pass beneath the railway, cross a bridge and take the arrowed footpath, to the right, before the second bridge.

❷ Walk beside the river, cross a footbridge and turn right. Cross a further footbridge and continue to a stile. Walk through water-meadows close to the river, go through a gate and maintain

BOX

WHILE YOU'RE THERE

Visit Hazelbury Manor at Wadswick (off B3109) for its restored, richly varied landscaped gardens, with stone and yew circles, a rockery, formal gardens, rose gardens and laburnum walk. Visit the heritage centre in Corsham to learn about the Bath stone quarrying industry.

direction. Shortly, bear left to a squeeze stile in the field corner. Follow the right-hand field-edge to a stile and lane.

❸ Turn right, then right again at the junction. Cross the river, pass Drewett's Mill and steeply ascend the lane. Just past Mills Platt Farm, take the arrowed footpath ahead across a stile. Continue steeply uphill to a stile and cross the A4. Ascend steps to a lane and proceed straight on up Barnetts Hill. Keep right at the fork, then right again and pass the Quarryman's Arms.

❹ Keep left at the fork and continue beside Box Hill Common to a junction. Take the bridleway straight ahead into woodland. Almost immediately, fork left and follow the path close to the woodland edge. As it curves

right into the beech wood, bear left and follow the path through the gap in the wall and then immediately right at the junction of paths.

❺ Follow the bridle path to a fork. Keep left, then turn right at the T-junction and take the path left to a stile. Cross a further stile and descend into Thorn Wood, following the stepped path to a stile at the bottom.

❻ Continue through scrub to a stile and turn right beside the fence to a wall stile. Bear right to a further stile, then bear left uphill to a stile and the A365. Cross over and follow the drive ahead. Where it curves left by stables, keep ahead along the arrowed path to a house. Climb a few steps, bear right to pass Washwell cottage and follow the drive uphill to a T-junction.

❼ Turn left, then on entering Henley, take the path right, across a stile. Follow the field-edge to a stile and descend through a paddock to a stile. Continue to a stile and gate.

❽ Follow the drive ahead, bear left at the garage and take the metalled path right, into Box. Cross the main road and continue to the A4. Turn right, then left down the access road back to Selwyn Hall.

WHAT TO LOOK OUT FOR

Explore Box and locate the Blind House on the main street, one of a dozen in Wiltshire for disturbers of the peace. Look for Coleridge House, named after the poet who often broke his journey here on his way to Nether Stowey. Also look for the former Candle Factory on the Rudloe road that once produced the candles used during the building of Box Tunnel, and head east along the A4 for the best view of the tunnel's entrance.

WHERE TO EAT AND DRINK

In Box, you will find both the Queen's Head and The Bear offer good food and ale in convivial surroundings. Time your walk for opening time at the Quarryman's Arms on Box Hill. Enjoy the views across Box from the dining room with a pint of locally brewed ale.

Corsham – a Wealthy Weaving Town

Explore this architectural treasure of a town and the adjacent Corsham Park.

DISTANCE *4 miles (6.4km)*   MINIMUM TIME *2hrs*

ASCENT/GRADIENT *114ft (35m)* ▲▲▲   LEVEL OF DIFFICULTY +++

PATHS *Field paths and country lanes, 10 stiles*

LANDSCAPE *Town streets, gently undulating parkland, farmland*

SUGGESTED MAP *OS Explorer 156 Chippenham & Bradford-on-Avon*

START / FINISH *Grid reference: ST 871704*

DOG FRIENDLINESS *Can be off lead in Corsham Park, except where grazing*

PARKING *Long-stay car park in Newlands Lane*

PUBLIC TOILETS *Short-stay car park by shopping precinct*

W arm, cream-coloured Bath stone characterises this handsome little market town on the southern edge of the Cotswolds. An air of prosperity pervades the streets where the 15th-century Flemish gabled cottages and baroque-pedimented 17th-century Hungerford Almshouses mix with larger Georgian residences. Architectural historian Nikolaus Pevsner wrote: 'Corsham has no match in Wiltshire for the wealth of good houses.' The town owes its inheritance to the once-thriving industries of cloth manufacture and stone quarrying in the 17th and 18th centuries.

Architectural Delights

Spend some time exploring the heart of the town before setting off across Corsham Park, as many of the fine stone buildings along the High Street, Church Street and Priory Street have been well preserved. Begin your town stroll at the Heritage Centre in the High Street (No 31), where interactive displays and hands-on exhibits present the stories of the weaving industry and quarrying of the golden Bath stone, which was used to create the architectural legacy of the town. In fact, No 31 once belonged to a prosperous 18th-century clothier, and No 70 (now an electrical shop) was the workhouse providing labour for the cloth industry. The Town Hall was formerly the market hall with one storey and open arches before being converted in 1882. North of the post office you will see the unspoilt line of 17th-century weavers' cottages. Known as the Flemish Buildings, this was the centre of the cloth industry where the Flemish weavers settled following religious persecution in their homeland. In Church Street, note the gabled cottages of the 18th-century weavers, with their ornate porches and a door on the first floor for taking in the raw wool.

Corsham Court – the Methuen Family Home

The finest of the houses is Corsham Court, a splendid Elizabethan mansion built in 1582 on the site of a medieval royal manor. It was bought in 1745 by Paul Methuen, a wealthy clothier and ancestor of the present owner, to house the family's collection of 16th- and 17th-century Italian and

CORSHAM

Flemish Master paintings and statuary. The house and park you see today are principally the work of 'Capability' Brown, John Nash and Thomas Bellamy. Brown built the gabled wings that house the state rooms and magnificent 72ft (22m) long picture gallery and laid out the park, including the avenues, Gothic bathhouse and the 13-acre (5ha) lake. Round off your walk with a tour of the house. You will see the outstanding collection of over 140 paintings, including pictures by Rubens, Turner, Reynolds and Van Dyck, fine statuary and bronzes, and the famous collection of English furniture, notably pieces by Robert Adam and Thomas Chippendale. You may recognise the house as the backdrop for the film *The Remains of the Day* (1993) starring Anthony Hopkins.

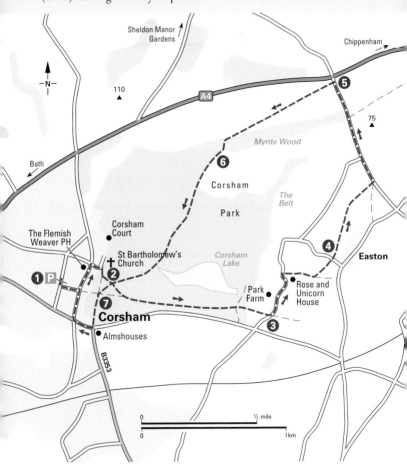

WALK 46 DIRECTIONS

❶ Turn left out of the car park, then left again along Post Office Lane to reach the High Street. Turn left, pass the tourist information centre and turn right into Church Street. Pass the

impressive entrance to Corsham Court, on your left, and enter St Bartholomew's churchyard.

❷ Follow the path left to a gate and walk ahead to join the main path across Corsham Park. Turn left and walk along the south side

CORSHAM

Corsham is well served by pubs, restaurants and cafés, notably The Flemish Weaver pub on the High Street, serving modern food and excellent Bath Ales.

WHILE YOU'RE THERE

Visit Sheldon Manor Gardens (3 miles/4.8km north), Wiltshire's oldest inhabited manor house and sole survivor of a deserted medieval village. Dating from 1282, this well-preserved Plantagenet house has been a family home for 700 years and features a 13th-century porch, a 15th-century chapel and beautiful informal terraced gardens.

of the park, passing Corsham Lake, to reach a stile and gate. Keep straight on along a fenced path beside a track to a kissing gate and proceed across a field to a stile and lane.

❸ Turn left, pass Park Farm, a splendid stone farmhouse on your left, and shortly take the waymarked footpath right along a drive to pass Rose and Unicorn House. Cross a stile and follow the right-hand field-edge to a stile, then bear half left to a stone stile in the field corner. Ignore the path arrowed right and head straight across the field to a further stile and lane.

❹ Take the footpath opposite, bearing half left to a stone stile to the left of a cottage. Maintain direction, passing to the right of a spring and go through a field entrance to follow the path along the left-hand side of a field to a stile in the corner. Turn left along the road for 0.5 mile (800m) to reach the A4.

❺ Go through the gate in the wall on your left and follow the worn path right, across the centre of parkland pasture to a metal kissing gate. Proceed ahead to reach a kissing gate on the edge of woodland. Follow the wide path to a further gate and bear half right to a stile.

❻ Keep ahead on a worn path across the parkland and along the field-edge to a gate. Continue to a further gate with fine views right to Corsham Court. Follow the path right along the field-edge, then where it curves right, bear left to join the path beside the churchyard wall to a stile.

❼ Turn left down the avenue of trees to a gate and the town centre, noting the stone almshouses on your left. Turn right along Lacock Road and then right again along the pedestrianised High Street. Turn left back along Post Office Lane to the car park.

WHAT TO LOOK OUT FOR

Note the Folly along Church Street, an artificial ruin, set with church windows, built by Nash in 1800 to hide Ethelred House from Corsham Court. Seek out the grave of Sarah Jarvis behind St Bartholomew's Church; she died in 1703 aged 107 having grown a new set of teeth! A plaque at 38 High Street informs that Sir Michael Tippett, one of Britain's greatest composers, lived there in the 1960s.

WALK 47

Lacock – the Birthplace of Photography

Combine a stroll around the medieval village with a riverside walk and a visit to Lacock Abbey, home of photographic pioneer Fox Talbot.

DISTANCE 5.5 miles (8.8km)   **MINIMUM TIME** 2hrs 30min

ASCENT/GRADIENT 426ft (130m) ▲▲▲   **LEVEL OF DIFFICULTY** ✦✦✦

PATHS Field paths and tracks; some road walking, 22 stiles

LANDSCAPE River valley, wooded hillside and parkland

SUGGESTED MAP OS Explorer 156 Chippenham & Bradford-on-Avon

START / FINISH Grid reference: ST 918682

DOG FRIENDLINESS Can be off lead on riverside pastures if free of cattle

PARKING Free car park on edge of Lacock

PUBLIC TOILETS Adjacent to Stables Tea Room in Lacock village

---

Timeless Lacock could stand as the pattern of the perfect English village with its twisting streets, packed with attractive buildings from the 15th to 18th centuries, possessing all the character and atmosphere of medieval England. Half-timbering, lichen grey stone, red-brick and whitewashed façades crowd together and above eye-level, uneven upper storeys, gabled ends and stone roofs blend with charming ease.

With the founding of an abbey in the 13th century, the village grew rich on the medieval wool industry and continued to prosper as an important coaching stop between Marlborough and Bristol until the mid-18th century when, as an estate-owned village, time seemed to stand still for nearly 100 years. Owned and preserved by the National Trust since 1944, Lacock is among England's most beautiful villages and is one of Wiltshire's most visited. If you're interested in architecture and plan to visit Lacock Abbey, allow the whole day to explore the village and enjoy this walk.

Fox Talbot and Lacock Abbey

Of all the outstanding buildings in the village Lacock Abbey, on the outskirts, is the most beautiful. It began as an Augustinian nunnery in 1232, but after the Reformation Sir William Sharrington used the remains to build a Tudor mansion, preserving the fine cloister court, sacristy and chapter house, and adding a romantic octagonal tower, courtyard and chimney stacks.

The abbey passed to the Talbot family through marriage and they Gothicised the south elevation and added the oriel windows. Surrounded by water-meadows bordering the River Avon, this was the setting for the experiments of William Henry Fox Talbot (1800–77), which in 1835 led to the creation of the world's first photographic negative. You can see some of Fox Talbot's work and equipment, alongside photographic exhibitions, in the beautifully restored 16th-century barn at the gates to the abbey.

Village Highlights

Architectural gems to note as you wander around Lacock's ancient streets include the timber-framed Sign of the Angel Inn, on Church Street, which retains its medieval layout, a 16th-century doorway and the passage through which horses would pass. Near by, Cruck House, with one of its cruck beams exposed, is a rare example of this 14th-century building method. Further along, you will pass King John's Hunting Lodge, reputed to be even older than the abbey, and St Cyriac's Church which contains the grandiose Renaissance tomb of Sir William Sharrington. In West Street, the George Inn dates back to 1361 and features a huge open fire with a dogwheel which was connected to the spit on the fire and turned by a dog called a Turnspit. Next door to the pub take a quick look at the bus shelter; it was formerly the village smithy.

On the corner of East Street is the magnificent 14th-century tithe barn with fine curved timbers. This was once used to store the rents which were paid to the abbey in kind, such as corn, hides and fleeces. The building later became the market hall as Lacock flourished into a thriving wool trading centre. Finally, don't miss the 18th-century domed lock-up next door. This is known as a 'blind house', since many of its overnight prisoners were drunks. You may recognise Lacock's medieval streets as the backdrop to several television costume dramas, notably Jane Austen's *Pride and Prejudice* (1995) and *Emma* (1996), and Daniel Defoe's bawdy *Moll Flanders* (1996).

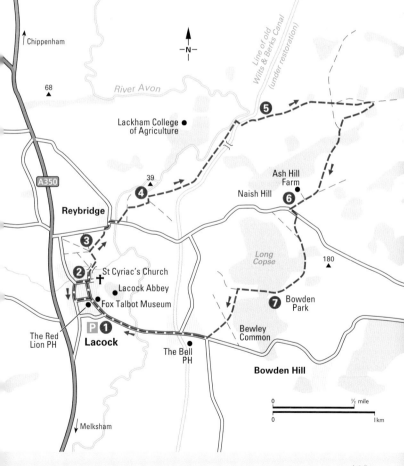

WALK 47 DIRECTIONS

1 From the car park, cross the road and follow the path into Lacock. Turn right into East Street opposite the Red Lion and walk down to Church Street. Turn left, then keep left into West Street and go left again into High Street. Walk back down East Street.

2 Turn right along Church Street and bear left in front of the church to cross a bridge over the Bide Brook. Follow the path by the stream then up the lane to the end of the road.

3 Go through the kissing gate on your right and follow the tarmac path across the field to a gate. Pass cottages to a lane, turn right, and then right again to cross the River Avon. Climb the stile on your left. Bear diagonally right across the field to a stile and cross the lane and stile opposite. Follow the path to two squeeze stiles and turn left around the field-edge.

4 Climb the stiles on your left and turn right along the field-edge. Follow the path through scrub to a stile and proceed ahead along a tarmac path beside the old Wilts and Berks Canal. Pass a restored bridge, then just before the second gate, cross the stile on the right and proceed to a further stile. Climb through trees and scrub to a stile, then follow the worn path half right and uphill along the field-edge to a gate.

5 Cross the next field to a gate, then keep ahead to cross a metalled farm drive and continue along the field edge to a gate. Ascend a grassy track to a gate and walk uphill towards a house. Before a gate, turn right across the top of the field to reach double stiles. Bear half right to a gate and ascend the farm drive through woodland, then uphill to a gate. Continue to a lane.

6 Turn left, then cross the stile on the right before a house. Keep to the left-hand field-edge, cross a stile and bear diagonally left to a stile in the field corner. Cross the stile ahead into woodland and continue to another stile. Proceed ahead along the field-edge to a stile on your right. Bear half left across Bowden Park, keeping to the right of a clump of trees, and bear right to a stile beside a gate.

7 Head downhill to a stile and turn left around the field-edge to a stile and gate near a house. Follow the path to the drive and follow it left. As tarmac gives way to gravel, bear off right across Bewley Common to the road. Turn right and return to Lacock.

A Canal and a Church at Bradford-on-Avon

Combine a visit to this enchanting riverside town and its surprising Saxon church, with a canal-side stroll.

DISTANCE 3.25 miles (5.3km)	**MINIMUM TIME** 1hr 45min

ASCENT/GRADIENT 164ft (50m) ▲▲▲   **LEVEL OF DIFFICULTY** ✦✦✦

PATHS *Tow path, field and woodland paths, metalled lanes*

LANDSCAPE *Canal, river valley, wooded hillsides, town streets*

SUGGESTED MAP *OS Explorer156 Chippenham & Bradford-on-Avon*

START / FINISH *Grid reference: ST 824606*

DOG FRIENDLINESS *On lead through town*

PARKING *Bradford-on-Avon Station car park (charge)*

PUBLIC TOILETS *Station car park*

Set in the wooded Avon Valley, Bradford is one of Wiltshire's loveliest towns, combining historical charm, appealing architecture and dramatic topography. It is often likened to a miniature Bath, the town sharing the same honey-coloured limestone, elegant terraces and steep winding streets that rise sharply away from the river. Historically a 'broad ford' across the Avon, the original Iron Age settlement was expanded in turn by the Romans and Saxons, the latter giving Bradford its greatest treasure, St Laurence's Church. The Avon was spanned by a fine stone bridge in the 13th century – two of its arches survive in the present 17th-century structure – and by the 1630s Bradford had grown into a powerful centre for the cloth and woollen industries.

Wealthy Wool Town

You will find exploring the riverside and the lanes, alleys and flights of steps up the north slope of the town most rewarding. Beautiful terraces are lined with elegant 18th-century merchants' houses with walled gardens, and charming 17th- and 18th-century weavers' cottages, the best examples being located along Newtown, Middle Rank and Tory terraces. The latter is the highest and affords superb views of the town. The wealth needed to make all this building possible came from the manufacture of woollen cloth. In the early 1700s Daniel Defoe, author of *Robinson Crusoe*, commented 'They told me at Bradford that it was no extra-ordinary thing to have clothiers in that county worth from £10,000 to £40,000 per man.' Bradford's medieval prosperity is reflected in the size of the magnificent 14th-century tithe barn at Barton Farm.

With the development of mechanisation, the wool trade moved from individual houses to large water and steam driven mills alongside the banks of the Avon. At the time that the Kennet and Avon Canal was built, in 1810, the town supported around 30 mills and some of these buildings survive, in various degrees of restoration or disrepair, today. With the centre of the wool trade shifting north to Yorkshire, the industry declined during the 19th century and the last of the mills closed in 1905. The town is now prosperous once again with tourists and new residents, many of them commuting to Bath, Bristol and even London.

Jewel in the Crown

Down by the river, the tiny, bare Saxon Church of St Laurence is the jewel in Bradford's crown and you really should not miss it! It was founded by St Aldhelm, the Abbot of Malmesbury, in AD 700 and this present structure dates from the 10th century. For centuries its presence was forgotten. The chancel became a house, the nave a school, and the west wall formed part of a factory building. The true origins and purpose of the site were only rediscovered in 1858 and, after careful restoration, it remains one of the best-preserved Saxon churches in England.

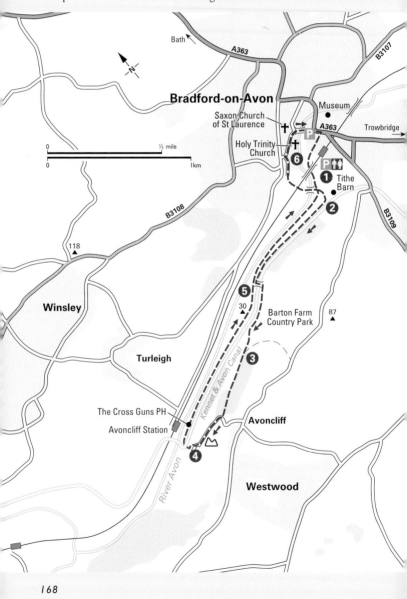

WALK 48 DIRECTIONS

1 Walk to the end of the car park, away from the station, and follow the path left beneath the railway and beside the River Avon. Enter Barton Farm Country Park and keep to the path across a grassy area to a junction of paths. With the packhorse bridge right, bear right, then left to pass to the right of the tithe barn to reach the Kennet and Avon Canal.

2 Turn right along the tow path, signed to Avoncliff. Cross the bridge over the canal in 0.5 mile (800m) and follow the path right to a footbridge and gate. Proceed along the right-hand field-edge to a further gate, then bear diagonally left uphill away from the canal to a kissing gate.

3 Follow the path through the edge of woodland. Keep to the path as it bears left uphill through the trees to reach a metalled lane. Turn right and walk steeply downhill to Avoncliff and the canal.

4 Don't cross the aqueduct, instead pass the Mad Hatter Tea Rooms, descend the steps on your right and pass beneath the canal. Keep right by The Cross Guns and join the tow path towards Bradford-on-Avon. Continue for 0.75 mile (1.2km) to the bridge passed on your outward route.

5 Bear off left downhill along a metalled track and follow it beside the River Avon back into Barton Farm Country Park. Cross the packhorse bridge and the railway and follow the walled path uphill and right into Barton Orchard. Bear right at the end down the alleyway to Church Street.

6 Continue ahead to pass the Holy Trinity Church and the Saxon Church of St Laurence. Cross the footbridge and walk through St Margaret's car park to the road. Turn right, then right again into the station car park.

Through the Avon and Frome Valleys

Combine a glorious walk through the beautiful Avon and Frome valleys with a visit to a romantic hillside garden at Iford Manor.

DISTANCE 3.5 miles (5.7km)   MINIMUM TIME 2hrs

ASCENT/GRADIENT 170ft (52m) ▲▲▲   LEVEL OF DIFFICULTY ✦✦✦

PATHS Riverside, field and woodland paths, metalled lanes, 5 stiles

LANDSCAPE Canal, river valley, wooded hillsides

SUGGESTED MAP OS Explorers 142 Shepton Mallet & Mendip
Hills East; 156 Chippenham & Bradford-on-Avon

START / FINISH Grid reference: ST 805599 (on Explorer 156)

DOG FRIENDLINESS No real problems

PARKING Avoncliff car park (free)

PUBLIC TOILETS None en route

Virtually every precious ingredient of the ever-changing countryside is included in this glorious walk from the Kennet and Avon Canal at Avoncliff to Freshford and the River Frome, and sleepy Iford on the Somerset border. The river scenery by the Avon and the Frome is surprisingly dramatic and, for good measure, there is a Tudor manor house at Iford with beautiful Italianate gardens. If that's not enough to satisfy you, then you can extend your walk along the canal tow path from Avoncliff to elegant Bradford-on-Avon, and return to Avoncliff by train.

Avoncliff Aqueduct

West of Bradford-on-Avon, the meandering River Avon is accompanied by the Kennet and Avon Canal as it passes through the dramatic and steeply wooded hillsides that rise 400ft (122m) above the river, arguably the finest natural landscape in west Wiltshire. Stretching 87 miles (140km) from Bristol to Reading, the Kennet and Avon Canal was built with great skill by the canal engineer John Rennie, opening in 1810 to carry goods to and from London. To negotiate the steep and winding Avon Valley, Rennie had to construct two substantial aqueducts, one of which you can see at Avoncliff. Built in 1804, it is 110yds (100m) long.

In the Frome Valley

Leaving the canalside, the walk enters the valley of the River Frome. On a steep hillside overlooking lush water-meadows and the confluence of the two rivers stands the attractive village of Freshford. It prospered in the early 19th century through the production of broadcloth and has some handsome stone houses and a popular riverside inn. You've passed into Somerset now, but the scenery is just as fine.

Iford Manor Gardens

Occupying a steep slope on the opposite bank of River Frome, the romantic gardens of Iford Manor, a fine Tudor mansion with a striking classical

AVONCLIFFE

front added in 1730, are a subtle blend of Italianate layout and English planting. This was the garden created by the distinguished architect and landscape designer, Harold Peto, who lived at Iford from 1899 to 1933. The topography of Iford lent itself to the strong architectural framework of steps, terraces and pools, and the predominant theme of the design is Italian, with plantings of cypress, juniper, box and yew interspersed with stone sarcophagi, urns, marble seats and statues, columns and loggias. You can see the unique and fascinating results of Peto's labours on selected days during the summer months.

Bradford-on-Avon

When you've completed this walk, it is well worth taking a leisurely stroll alongside the Kennet and Avon Canal into the heart of Bradford-on-Avon (See Walk 48), where you will find houses of Bath stone, built between the 16th and 18th centuries, rising steeply above the River Avon in a town made prosperous by Dutch weavers. A wander through the town will reveal its splendid 14th-century tithe barn, one of the largest to have been built in England, and the town's most historic landmark, the tiny Saxon Church of St Laurence which dates from about 700.

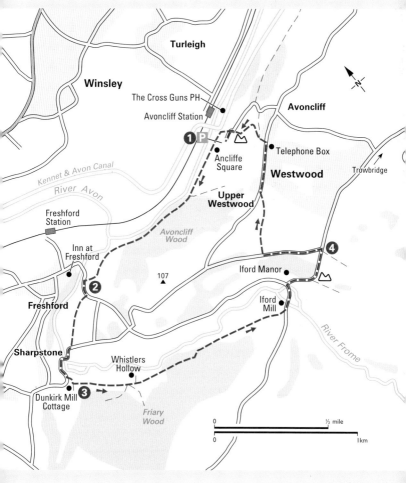

WALK 49 DIRECTIONS

❶ Turn left out of the car park. drop down past the Mad Hatter Tea Rooms on your left, disregard the tow path signs and keep ahead along the track to pass Ancliffe Square. As it veers left, maintain your direction through the gate and trees. Go through a gate and soon walk beside the River Avon to reach another gate. Pass through woodland to a gate, then head across water-meadows to a gate and lane and the River Frome at Freshford.

WHAT TO LOOK OUT FOR

At Avoncliff you can see weavers' cottages and two flock mills (one a ruin the other converted to a house) that stand upstream either side of the weir below Rennie's fine aqueduct. On your outward route, just beyond the tea rooms at Avoncliff, you'll see the old workhouse (Ancliffe Square) which is now modern apartments.

❷ Turn left, climb a stile on your right and bear half left across the field towards a derelict factory, to a stile and lane. Turn right, walk beside the river and cross the bridge. Continue uphill and take the bridle path left in front of Dunkirk Mill Cottage. Bear right, then take the bridle path left opposite Middle House.

❸ Continue to a gate, keep left down to a track and turn left.

Turn right opposite a house called Whistlers Hollow, to a stile and gate. Keep left through a field to another stile and walk through Friary Wood to a stile. Turn right along the field-edge for 0.5 mile (800m) to a stile and lane. Turn left, pass Iford Mill and cross the river bridge to Iford Manor Gardens. Bear right and walk steeply uphill to a junction.

❹ Turn left along the verge for 0.25 mile (400m) and take the bridle path right, signed 'Upper Westwood'. At a lane, turn right through Upper Westwood. Turn left opposite the telephone box then, where the lane curves left, take the left of two footpaths ahead. Walk downhill through the edge of woodland. Go through a gate, cross a drive and follow the lane left, downhill back to Avoncliff and the car park.

EXTENDING THE WALK

You can combine this walk with Walk 48 which will take you into the town of Bradford-on-Avon, barely a mile (1.6km) upriver.

WHERE TO EAT AND DRINK

At Avoncliff, The Cross Guns offers traditional pub food and a terraced riverside garden. The Mad Hatter Tea Rooms serve lunches. Enjoy a pint at the Inn at Freshford or home-made teas at the Peto Gardens at Iford Manor (summer weekends and bank holidays only).

WHILE YOU'RE THERE

Two miles (3.2km) south-east is Westwood Manor, a fully furnished 15th-century stone manor with original Gothic and Jacobean windows and fine plasterwork. In Bradford-on-Avon, discover the natural and historical heritage of the town with a visit to the town's fascinating museum. At Barton Farm Country Park, view the craft shops in the former medieval farm buildings and marvel at the great beams and rafters of Bradford's magnificent, cathedral-like tithe barn, the second largest in Britain.

A Walk with Good Manors from Holt

Stroll from a rare industrial village to a beautiful moated manor house.

DISTANCE *3 miles (4.8km)*   **MINIMUM TIME** *1hr 30min*

ASCENT/GRADIENT *147ft (45m)* ▲▲▲   **LEVEL OF DIFFICULTY** ✚✚✚

PATHS *Field paths, metalled track, country lanes, 6 stiles*

LANDSCAPE *Gently undulating farmland*

SUGGESTED MAP *OS Explorer 156 Chippenham & Bradford-on-Avon*

START / FINISH *Grid reference: ST 861619*

DOG FRIENDLINESS *Keep dogs under control at all times*

PARKING *Holt Village Hall car park*

PUBLIC TOILETS *Only if visiting The Courts or Great Chalfield Manor*

Threaded by the busy B3107 linking Melksham to Bradford-on-Avon, Holt is a rare industrial Wiltshire village with a significant history as a cloth-making and leather-tanning centre. The tannery, founded in the early 18th century, still occupies the main three-storey factory in the appropriately named small industrial area – The Midlands – while bedding manufacture and light engineering now occupy former cloth factories. Holt also enjoyed short-lived fame between 1690 and 1750 as a spa, based on the curative properties of a spring, but its popularity declined in face of competition from nearby Bath. The most attractive part of the village is at Ham Green where elegant 17th- and 18th-century houses stand along three sides of a fine green shaded by horse chestnut trees, and a quiet lane leads to the late Victorian parish church with a Perpendicular tower.

The Courts – Wiltshire's Secret Garden

From the green a walled walk leads to The Courts, a substantial 18th-century house that served, as its name suggests, as the place where the local magistrate sat to adjudicate in the disputes of the cloth weavers from Bradford-on-Avon. Although not open, the house makes an attractive backdrop to 7 acres (2.8ha) of authentic English country garden owned by the National Trust. Hidden away behind high walls and reached through an avenue of pleached limes, you will find a series of garden 'rooms'. Stroll along a network of stone paths through formal gardens featuring yew topiary, lawns with colourful herbaceous borders, a lake and lily pond with aquatic and water-tolerant plants, and explore an area given over to wild flowers among an interesting small arboretum of trees and shrubs.

Great Chalfield Manor

You will glimpse the Tudor chimneys and gabled windows of this enchanting manor house as you stride across peaceful field paths a mile (1.6km) or so north-west of Holt. Enhanced by a moat and gatehouse, this exquisite group of buildings will certainly live up to your expectations and really must be visited. Built in 1480, during the Wars of the Roses, by Thomas Tropenell,

HOLT

Great Chalfield is one of the most perfect examples of the late medieval English manor house which, with its adjacent church, mill, great barn and other Elizabethan farm buildings, makes a harmonious visual group.

Sensitively restored in the early 20th century by Sir Harold Brakspear after two centuries of neglect and disrepair, the manor house is centred on its traditional great hall, which rises to the rafters and is lit by windows, including two beautiful oriels, positioned high in the walls. Join one of the guided tours and you will be able to see the fine vaulting, the chimney place of the hall, the concealed spy-holes in the gallery, designed to allow people to see what was going on in the great hall, and the amusing ornaments, gargoyles and other fascinating details of this fine building.

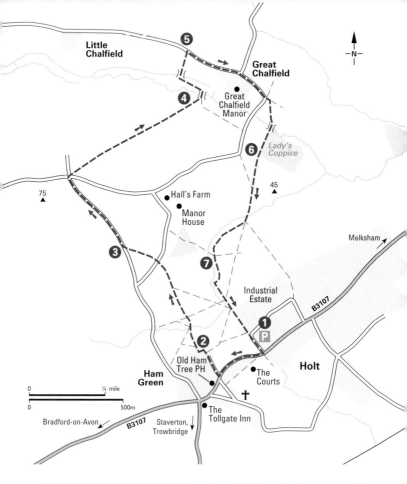

WALK 50 DIRECTIONS

❶ Turn left out of the car park and then right along the B3107 through the village. Just before the Old Ham Tree pub, turn right along Ground Corner. At the end of the lane take the waymarked path left along a drive. Follow the fenced path beside Highfields to a kissing gate.

❷ Keep to the right along the edge of the field, then keep

ahead in the next field towards the clump of fir trees. Continue following the worn path to the right, into a further field. Keep left along the field-edge to a stile in the top corner. Maintain direction to a ladder stile and cross the metalled drive and stile opposite. Bear diagonally left through the field to a hidden stile in the hedge, level with the clump of trees to your right.

❸ Turn right along the lane. At a junction, turn right towards Great Chalfield and go through the kissing gate almost immediately on your left. Take the arrowed path right, diagonally across a large field towards Great Chalfield Manor visible ahead.

❹ Go through a gate and bear half right down to another gate. Cross a footbridge over the stream, then a stile and bear diagonally left over the field to a gate. Cross the bridge and go ahead beside the hedge to a metalled track by a barn.

❺ Turn right, then right again when you reach the lane, passing in front of Great Chalfield Manor. At the sharp right-hand bend, go through the gate ahead and bear right, then half left across the field to cross a footbridge over a stream. Continue walking straight on up the field beside woodland to reach a gate in the field corner.

❻ Follow the left-hand field-edge to a gate, then follow the path straight ahead towards a chimney on the skyline. Go through a gate, bear immediately right to a gate in the hedge and turn right along the path around the field edge.

❼ Ignore the stile on your right and continue to the field corner and a raised path beside water. Go through a gate and turn left along the field-edge to a further gate on your left. Join the drive past Garland Farm and pass between small factory buildings to the road and turn right back to the car park.

Walking in Safety

All these walks are suitable for any reasonably fit person,
but less experienced walkers should try the easier walks first.
Route finding is usually straightforward, but you will find that an
Ordnance Survey map is a useful addition to the route maps and
descriptions.

RISKS

Although each walk here has been researched with a view to
minimising the risks to the walkers who follow its route, no walk in
the countryside can be considered to be completely free from risk.
Walking in the outdoors will always require a degree of common
sense and judgement to ensure that it is as safe as possible.

- Be particularly careful on cliff paths and in upland terrain,
  where the consequences of a slip can be very serious.

- Remember to check tidal conditions before walking on the
  seashore.

- Some sections of route are by, or cross, busy roads. Take care
  and remember traffic is a danger even on minor country lanes.

- Be careful around farmyard machinery and livestock, especially
  if you have children with you.

- Be aware of the consequences of changes in the weather and
  check the forecast before you set out. Carry spare clothing and
  a torch if you are walking in the winter months. Remember the
  weather can change very quickly at any time of the year, and
  in moorland and heathland areas, mist and fog can make route
  finding much harder. Don't set out in these conditions unless
  you are confident of your navigation skills in poor visibility. In
  summer remember to take account of the heat and sun; wear a
  hat and carry spare water.

- On walks away from centres of population you should carry a
  whistle and survival bag. If you do have an accident requiring the
  emergency services, make a note of your position as accurately
  as possible and dial 999.

COUNTRYSIDE CODE

- Be safe, plan ahead and follow any signs.

- Leave gates and property as you find them.

- Protect plants and animals and take your litter home.

- Keep dogs under close control.

- Consider other people.

For more information visit www.countrysideaccess.gov.uk/things_
to_know/countryside_code